British Architecture: A Very Short Introduction

VERY SHORT INTRODUCTIONS are for anyone wanting a stimulating and accessible way into a new subject. They are written by experts, and have been translated into more than 45 different languages.

The series began in 1995, and now covers a wide variety of topics in every discipline. The VSI library currently contains over 750 volumes—a Very Short Introduction to everything from Psychology and Philosophy of Science to American History and Relativity—and continues to grow in every subject area.

Very Short Introductions available now:

Available soon:

For more information visit our website

www.oup.com/vsi/

Dana Arnold

BRITISH
ARCHITECTURE

A Very Short Introduction

OXFORD
UNIVERSITY PRESS

OXFORD
UNIVERSITY PRESS

Great Clarendon Street, Oxford, OX2 6DP,
United Kingdom

Oxford University Press is a department of the University of Oxford.
It furthers the University's objective of excellence in research, scholarship,
and education by publishing worldwide. Oxford is a registered trade mark of
Oxford University Press in the UK and in certain other countries

Published in the United States of America by Oxford University Press
198 Madison Avenue, New York, NY 10016, United States of America

British Library Cataloguing in Publication Data
Data available

Library of Congress Control Number: 2023948863

ISBN 978-0-19-289821-0

Printed and bound by
CPI Group (UK) Ltd, Croydon, CR0 4YY

For Nigel

Contents

Preface

This book aims to present an original and engaging introduction to the rich and diverse nature of the architecture of the British Isles. Avoiding the traditional approach of a chronological survey of architects and architectural style, each of the chapters presents a thematic, jargon-free exploration of key aspects of British architecture that endure across time and that still have relevance today. Focussing on medieval times to the present day, the book enables the reader to appreciate the artistic and cultural significance of British architecture and how it operates as a barometer of social trends. We also see the ways in which architecture can project national and regional identities.

British architecture tells of the perceived nature of Britishness and is an important means of understanding Britain's connection with the rest of the world. There is no doubt about the international significance of the work of recent and contemporary British architects—their 'star' buildings are a dominant feature of cityscapes across the globe. And a thematic, historical understanding of British architecture in terms of its form and purpose explains much about the society and culture it was built for, and its legacy for subsequent generations. We learn how a preoccupation with the past has been a constant theme in design thinking and practice. Equally, debates about how best to express the nationhood through its architecture reveal much about

Britain's perception of itself and its relationship with the world. We also see how architecture continues to shape patterns of living and social interaction, and responds to new demands. Developments in building materials and engineering techniques, and the ways in which architecture engages with nature and the environment reveal important trends in design thinking across a broad sweep of time.

The opening chapter addresses the questions of what is understood by the term British architecture and how it has changed over time with regard to indigenous and foreign influences. It explores the ways in which British architecture is distinctive across the regions and nations within the British Isles, as well as in a global context. It also provides a historical framework for the thematic exploration of British architecture in the chapters that follow. Of particular interest here are the questions of class and culture that are traced in the move from master mason to the gentleman architect, and eventually to the formalization of architecture as a profession. The aim here is to expand the idea of the architect from being solely white and male. Instead, we see architectural practice as a more inclusive category that comprises women, even before they were admitted to architecture schools, and more recently ethnic minorities. Perhaps most importantly, the chapter explains that architecture is not frozen in time; buildings are remodelled and extended, their function and surroundings may change. This introduces the broader question of how the historiography of British architecture has changed over time and the ways in which we can think differently about it.

The love of the past is an enduring theme in British architecture and this is explored in the second chapter. We look at how architecture from the past has been viewed and used to project national identity. In addition, we think about the ways in which buildings and their histories may have different meanings to a diverse range of publics. Revivals of classical and Gothic architecture have been particularly popular, especially in the 18th and the 19th centuries. But we find that the reasons behind these individual revivals were different and resulted in buildings that are quite distinctive in their re-interpretation of the architecture of the past. Such was the enthusiasm for the classical past that the image of whole cities was recast. We also see how the romantic view of former times extended beyond architectural style to represent sets of social and cultural values.

The idea of home is an architectural concept familiar to all of us. My third chapter explores examples ranging from the medieval hall to the high rise flat, this chapter examines the different types and attitudes towards housing in Britain. We see that there are common threads across the centuries, some of which might have been anticipated, others not, enabling us to make unexpected connections. The importance of both privacy and green space is intrinsic to our understanding of the idea of a home, no matter how grand or modest it may be. Perhaps more complex is what the density of dwellings both in terms of occupancy and their proximity to each other reveals about the relationship between housing and social class. We also see how architecture has accommodated patterns of living for a diverse range of occupants across centuries and social divides.

Britain's architectural relationship with the world can be explored on many levels. In the fourth chapter we look at the longstanding tradition of the porosity between British architecture and the rest of Europe. We also consider how British architecture was established as a presence in the world well before the work of star architects such as Zaha Hadid, Norman Foster, and Richard Rogers. The fifth chapter also introduces the theme of the projection of national identity in a global context not only through Britain's colonialist expansion but also in the architectural design of festivals and exhibitions held at home. This final chapter also reflects on the shifting nature of architectural practice as evidenced in this book and on the changes in our understanding and definition of the profession of architect, especially as it gradually evolves to become a more inclusive category.

Inevitably, the choice of examples in a short introduction to such a vast topic has to be selective. Indeed, I am conscious that the term British is not without its historical and present-day contentions. As a consequence, I use the term here fully cognisant of the shifting political and national geographies of the British Isles. Most importantly, while embracing these caveats, my intention is to open up possible avenues for further exploration and to provoke different ways of thinking about British architecture, in all its complexities.

Acknowledgements

The opportunity to write this *Very Short Introduction* came at a time when the history of British architecture was entering a period of revision. This ongoing process has resulted in long-established interpretations of buildings being re-evaluated. Consequently, the meaning of architecture has become more fluid, speaking to different publics in different ways at different points in time. As an architectural historian who has always sought to question canonical norms, the privilege of writing an introduction to the discipline that I have been so closely involved with in all its complexities was an irresistible challenge. This book seeks to sum up some of the ways in which our understanding of British architecture from across a broad sweep of time has developed in recent years, as well as identifying new ways in which we can appreciate its significance. I aim to cover the broadest possible spectrum of British architecture, ranging from grand well-known buildings to examples and building types that may be less familiar. The choices I had to make in terms of the approach, material covered, and which illustrations to use were the most enjoyable and most difficult part of writing this book. I was fortunate to be inspired and encouraged by many friends and colleagues in the preparation of this volume and, although any omissions or errors are my own, I would especially like to thank Andrew Ballantyne, Diane G. Favro, Adrian Rifkin, and Nancy Stieber for providing such stimulating and collegial conversations. I am also indebted to

Clare Barry for her assistance with the sourcing and selection of the illustrations. My thanks also go to my editors Latha Menon and Imogene Haslam, and to my project manager Kripadevi Prabhakar. Most of all I would like to thank Nigel King for his unstinting support and enthusiasm for my writing, and especially this book. Nigel's strength and elegance in the face of whatever life has thrown at him is to be completely admired. This book is for him.

Dana Arnold
London, 2023

List of illustrations

Chapter 1
What do we mean by British architecture?

What is architecture? And what makes it British? In answer to the first question, the renowned 20th-century architectural historian Sir Nikolaus Pevsner in his *Outline of European Architecture* (1943) famously remarked that 'a bicycle shed is a building; Lincoln Cathedral is a piece of architecture'. He goes on to observe that 'Nearly everything that encloses space on a scale sufficient for a human being to move in is a building; the term architecture applies only to buildings designed with a view to aesthetic appeal'. I wonder if these statements are entirely true, and if this is a helpful way of thinking about British architecture. In this *Very Short Introduction*, I explore the question of what is understood by the term British architecture and how it has developed and changed as regards its indigenous and foreign influences, with a focus on the medieval to modern periods. The chapters explore the ways in which British architecture is distinctive across the regions and nations within the British Isles, as well as in a global context.

My aim in this introductory chapter is to provide a framework for the thematic exploration of British architecture in the chapters that follow. I use specific examples as a kind of set of chronological stepping stones into British architecture. Running in parallel to this, I will also introduce some of the key writings that inform our knowledge of this vast topic. This in turn will highlight the different ways in which histories of British architecture have been written, and how these approaches influence our understanding of it. At the same time, I will raise important issues and questions that will appear throughout the book, beginning with the idea of the architect and whether architecture needs architects. More broadly, we will consider the ways in which we encounter architecture and what we value in British architecture beyond its specific style. Most importantly, we will explore how we can make British architecture more inclusive and representative of wider communities and publics.

Idea of the architect

What do we mean by the term architect? Our fascination with named architects certainly promotes the idea of the architect as sole creator and genius. This is linked in part to the preoccupation of architectural historians with identifying the designer of a building as an integral part of the process of historical investigation. Following on from this, there is a tendency to think that if a building has a named architect, it has greater significance than those with anonymous authors. This approach to thinking about architecture has informed the ways that many histories have been written. In turn these histories have established a distinct set of values with which to form a judgement about quality. A good example of this trend is Sir Howard Colvin's *Biographical Dictionary of British Architects 1600–1840* (1954). As the title suggests, this is an alphabetical survey of architects practising in Britain during this period. Their known works are divided into types and then listed in chronological order. If a building does not have a named architect, it is not included in the dictionary.

This view of the importance of the profession, and linked to it the genius of individual practitioners, has been fundamental to architectural history in Britain. Indeed, Colvin's agenda could not be more obvious in this regard. In his introductory essay to the dictionary, he sets out the relationship between biography and professionalism:

> It is appropriate to begin a biographical dictionary of professional men by giving some account of the history of their profession. Indeed, the history of British architecture is bound up with its own practice, and the careers of those architects and master workmen who figure in this dictionary would scarcely be intelligible without some idea of the conditions under which they designed and built...

Following on from this, Colvin sets out to trace the rise of the architectural profession in Britain, which he situates within the temporal parameters of his dictionary. He contends that in 1600 there were no architects in the sense in which we understand the term today. But by 1840 there was an established architectural profession, based on a regular system of pupillage. The Institute of British Architects, founded in 1834, was an important step in formalizing the profession, as it initiated a register of members who were recognized architects. Colvin traces the prehistory of this register and he sees the emergence of architecture as a profession as the result of the efforts and aspirations of the men listed in his volume. Their careers were, for Colvin, intertwined with the development of the professional architect. There is no doubt that the dictionary is an invaluable source of information about architects and their buildings during the period 1600–1840 and is presented in an easy-to-use alphabetical list format rather than as a chronological survey. However, the effect of this approach is to have established a value system for British architecture that ties it to its male architects, and to my mind this is a rather limited interpretation that I would like to unravel. Throughout this book, I will explore how British architecture is in fact far more inclusive and offers much richer layers of interpretation.

Let's see if thinking about the persona of the architect helps us with the conundrum of Lincoln Cathedral versus the bicycle shed (see Figure 1). Lincoln's building history spans several centuries, including reconstructions and expansion, and the present-day cathedral is the result of the endeavours of many actors. Conversely, at first glance a bicycle shed is usually considered as a utilitarian, purely functional structure without a named designer. But we need to dig a little deeper into Pevsner's provocative juxtaposition. First, let's consider the building history of Lincoln Cathedral and what we know of the personalities involved.

There is no doubt that Lincoln Cathedral is one of the largest and most important examples of medieval architecture in Western Europe. Most of its Gothic structure dates from the 13th century. But the built fabric has undergone significant subsequent alterations that show us how dynamic the history of architecture can be. The cathedral is the seat of the Anglican bishop of Lincoln. Its construction began in 1072 and continued in several phases throughout the High Middle Ages and beyond. The many building and rebuilding phases are linked to the various bishops, some of whom used the cathedral to express their ambitions, both religious and secular, while others led reconstructions as a result of a fire in 1124, and a devastating earthquake in 1185. The latter rebuilding and expansion of Lincoln Cathedral was overseen by Bishop Hugh de Burgundy, who became known as St Hugh of Lincoln. He had no experience of practising architecture but his expansive vision was undoubtedly important for the development of the cathedral. The nearest we have to an architect in this building phase is the master mason who supervised the building works.

Robert Grosseteste, bishop of Lincoln Cathedral in 1235–53, adds a new chapter to the building's history. Under his aegis, some of the vaults are attributed to the Norman-French master mason, Geoffrey de Noiers. And this is indicative of the cross-over between French and British architecture at this time in terms of

1. Lincoln Cathedral, Lincoln (1072 onwards).

design and the craftsmen used. De Noiers was succeeded by
Alexander the Mason, who developed the cathedral's examples of
more elaborate vaulting systems, as well as the Galilee Porch in
1249, built to provide a more regal entrance for the bishop's
ceremonial procession. Grosseteste also offers us a different view
of its architectural importance. A prolific author and gifted
scholar of philosophy, science, and cosmology, Grosseteste's
writings show us how the forms and spaces of the cathedral
related to medieval ideas about light and geometry, as well as the
cultural, religious, and political life of the period. The building
history of Lincoln continues into the 14th century with the
completion of the 160 metre (520 feet) high central spire in 1311.
The exceptional height of the spire made the cathedral one of the
tallest known buildings until it collapsed in 1548; it was not
rebuilt.

Parts of the cathedral's medieval structure have been lost; for
example, in 1673 the cloisters were described as 'ruinous', and so
were partially demolished in order to make space for the Wren

5

Library, designed by Sir Christopher Wren, begun in 1674 and finished around 1676. In 1724, the classical architect James Gibbs advised that the West Tower spires be removed due to these structural problems but his advice was not acted upon until 1807. The cathedral has continued to impress scholars throughout the ages. Notably, the 19th-century writer and critic John Ruskin declared: 'I have always held...that the cathedral of Lincoln is out and out the most precious piece of architecture in the British Isles and roughly speaking worth any two other cathedrals we have'. And this statement may be literally true as its footprint was indeed large—spreading over 5,000 square metres (approximately 54,000 square feet), which makes it one of the largest in Britain. Returning to Pevsner's dictum, we can see that Lincoln certainly meets his criteria as a work of architecture. The aesthetic is a driving force in its design throughout its evolution, even though this imposing medieval structure was realized without there being a persona of the kind we would now identify as an architect. The extended building history of Lincoln Cathedral and the various actors involved lead me to my next question—does architecture need architects?

Does architecture need architects?

The masons of the vaults at Lincoln are perhaps an example of a moment when individual 'actors' or groups of like-minded individuals can be identified as effecting significant changes in the approach to design. But are they architects? Spiro Kostof in his study of the architectural profession *The Architect: Chapters in the History of the Profession* (1977) extends Colvin's idea of the emergence of the persona of the architect being aligned with genius. Helpfully here, Kostof covers a much broader sweep of time. 'Architecture cannot be the world's oldest profession—tradition has decided that issue long ago—but its antiquity is not in doubt. The presence of architects is documented as far back as the third millennium before Christ.' Kostof argues that architects are conceivers of buildings who supply concrete images for new structures. Their primary task is to communicate what proposed buildings should be and should look like. As a consequence, architects do not necessarily take part in the physical act of construction, rather their role is that of mediator between the client or patron and those who carry out the construction work. This kind of architecture is sometimes referred to by the terms 'high' or 'polite' architecture, which imply qualitative judgements. Kostof goes on to distinguish two categories of buildings that in his view do not require architects. First, structures he calls 'standardised' buildings, which are produced by builders without the intervention of an architect for a general market. Second, Kostof identifies what is usually referred to as vernacular architecture, which is described as the result of individual efforts—people who decide to build, settle for the common look of the community, and produce buildings in this accepted local way. And these two categories of architecture together with architect-designed buildings are recurrent themes in this book.

I want now to step back to 16th-century Britain; a point in historical time not covered by Colvin's *Dictionary* or Kostof's professionalizing agenda; to a moment when the 'architect' was emerging as a recognized practitioner in the building process, as seen in building accounts and commentaries. This follows on from our consideration of Lincoln Cathedral to provide another chronological stepping stone through the history of British architecture. Here the persona of Robert Smythson provides a case study of the relationship between the evidence and the will of the historian to provide a particular sequence of biographical narrative and architectural historical analysis. This begins to reveal how, at an early stage in the formation of the canon of architectural history of the British Isles, the ability to identify and name an architect was important in placing limits or pause marks on the chronology of history. Architecture can be seen as 'emerging' from the 'dark ages' of relative anonymity, as we have seen at Lincoln, to the lightness of the named designer. In this way the notion of genius is explored through an individual architect.

How typical is Smythson's place in the schematic view of architectural history?

Robert Smythson was active at a time when the profession of architect was not clearly defined and the emergence of the architect as distinct from a craftsman was very much in its early stages. Smythson is a problematic and enigmatic figure who was involved in some capacity with the production of several Elizabethan 'great houses' (we might now describe these as country houses), including Longleat (1568–80) for Sir John Thynne, Wollaton Hall (1580–8) for Sir Francis Willoughby, and Hardwick Hall (1590–7) for Elizabeth, Countess of Shrewsbury, who was known as Bess of Hardwick. The late 16th century is often described as the moment when architecture in Britain began to emerge from the 'Middle Ages' and respond to the developments in Renaissance Europe. Smythson's work provides extant examples of this step change in architectural practice. An important factor here is the increased use of drawings on paper (rather than re-usable surfaces commonly found in earlier design practice) to work out the evolution of a design. Smythson's extant drawings allow us to trace the design process of some of his buildings and to speculate about his sources. The differing views of Smythson by key historians of the Elizabethan period show both the concern with the mapping of the emergence of the architect and an emphasis on biography. Smythson's career began at Longleat where, rather like the builders of Lincoln Cathedral, he was employed as a mason. Yet he has been described both as a 'working mason and professional surveyor of building operations' and as 'one of the great geniuses of English architecture'. Malcolm Airs in his book *The Making of the English Country House, 1500–1640* (1975) assessed Smythson thus:

> Robert Smythson worked for Thynne [the owner of Longleat] for
> twelve years starting in 1568. He was employed as one of the two
> principal masons, and there was no indication in the very full
> documentation for the building that he took any part in the

administration other than supervising the other masons in his own gang. He was, however, a workman of considerable experience and reputation...

We find a contrasting view in Mark Girouard's *Robert Smythson & the Elizabethan Country House* (1983).

Not only do the houses with which he [Robert Smythson] can be connected include some of the most important and impressive of their period; they were also full of ideas, new or newly expressed, which were taken up and developed elsewhere in the country. There is little doubt that Robert Smythson was one of the creators of the Elizabethan style.

The prodigy houses, as these grand country houses are often called, are exciting and original creations and can cause a problem for historians as they are geographically dispersed, have a range of patrons, and each has its own distinct aesthetic. They are impressive, significant works of architecture and it is desirable to be able to ascribe this achievement to an individual architect. But as we can see, historians have different views of Smythson not least on how Smythson made the leap from mason to architect. Given the physical distance between houses such as Wollaton and Hardwick, it is also probable that Smythson worked with different teams of builders whose ability and/or willingness to execute his designs might have varied. This ruffles Kostof's tidy view that architects are responsible for the aesthetics of a building and act as mediators between patron and builder. And Smythson is up against some very colourful patrons so it is tempting to see the architectural distinctiveness of their houses as representative of their differing personalities. For example, Bess of Hardwick, the patron of Hardwick Hall, was closely involved in the design of the building and indeed all matters architectural, including her own tomb (also worked on by Smythson). This seems a good moment to pause and reflect on the established traditions of the design of domestic architecture in Britain, and to think about the ways in which houses such as Hardwick both evolved from and disrupted these norms.

First we must consider the domestic architecture, especially the castles and fortified manor houses, that existed in Britain since the Norman Conquest. Examples from across all four nations share characteristics of imposing size and defensibility as well as formal elements including the great hall and the tower, both of which can be traced back to Roman precedents. Of particular interest here is the form of the great hall which evolved over centuries to serve the functional, ceremonial, and symbolic needs of the medieval household in dwellings of large and more modest scales. Typically, the larger rural medieval house comprised a hall at the centre which was single-storeyed and open to the roof. A service end was divided from the hall by a cross-passage at one end and the more private rooms were located at the other end, being accessed by stairs or ladders. This internal arrangement limited access by establishing a series of barriers and checkpoints for visitors entering the household, as only the master of the household had access to all the spaces. Once in the hall, the ample light from the large windows, the raised dais, the unbroken sight lines, and the high vaulted ceiling created the ideal stage for the performance of rituals of service and hospitality, leaving guests with a forceful impression of power and authority. The need for active military defence of land and property decreased during the Tudor regime, and with it the old feudal order that had led to very large households with complex hierarchies of occupants. The great house changed from a feudal defensive structure to representing a different set of social and cultural values. Consequently, the exterior style and interior layout changed substantially. Households became smaller and a different type of patron began to build country residences, both for leisure and as sites of display. And here we find a developing interest in Italian Renaissance architecture on the part of both architects and craftsmen, and their educated patrons.

The work of the Veneto architect Andrea Palladio, who publicized his own designs and provided a systematic guide to the architecture of Roman antiquity in his well-illustrated *Four Books of Architecture* (1570), is of special note here. Indeed, for more than two centuries, the *Four Books* maintained their position as one of the most influential sources for British architecture. The effect of Italian design on British architecture initially happened slowly. It began with the inclusion of isolated ornamental elements of Italianate classicism in the design of 16th-century great houses, but these were superficial decorative elements. By contrast, the highly specialized form of the hall with its aura of authority expressed through the ordered symmetries and open spaces of the axial or central plan was largely retained. Indeed, Wollaton Hall (1580–8), built by Smythson for Sir Francis Willoughby, is an important transitional example of this phenomenon. And it is from this commission that Smythson moved on to work for Bess of Hardwick, who, after Queen Elizabeth I, was the richest woman in England. Hardwick Hall was one of her many houses, and it was intended as a conspicuous statement of her wealth and power (Figure 2). Hardwick is a very distinctive house; perhaps most notable is the extensive use of glass in the many exceptionally large windows, which was then an expensive luxury. This distinct aesthetic required a technical innovation to ensure the structure was sound, so the chimneys were built into the internal walls of the building rather than on the exterior walls. At Hardwick, the hall became an open room entered directly from the front door, with a waist-high screen dividing off a lobby rather than the traditional passage. Only the lower servants ate meals here; the upper servants (unusually, they were mostly women) had separate-sex dining rooms on the second floor, adjacent to Bess's own. Thus, while the hall remained at the centre of the house, the more prestigious spaces moved above ground floor level. In this way, Hardwick is distinct among Elizabethan and Jacobean country houses for the rationality of its design. The three storeys of the house were each designed to accommodate a different sort of activity: the ground floor was

2. Hardwick Hall, Derbyshire (1590–7).

primarily devoted to service, the middle floor to the everyday needs of the mistress and her upper servants, and the top floor to formal entertainment, estate business, and state occasions.

The design of Hardwick was influenced by contemporary European classical architecture, especially that of Italy, France, and the Netherlands. Knowledge of this style was gleaned through travel by a privileged few but became more widely available through the increasing number of treatises and pattern books published in both Europe and Britain. Notable here is Palladio's influence on the system of rational, symmetrical planning and functional organization of space. We see this in the way that Smythson observed the axial planning of the ground plan, and made the house more compact and taller than his previous buildings. Each of the three main storeys has a higher ceiling than the one below, the ceiling height being indicative of the importance of the rooms' occupants: the least noble being at the bottom and the grandest at the top.

Bess's letters give us a very full picture of her understanding and engagement with architecture at a variety of levels, from practical maintenance to issues of the aesthetics of a design. She appreciated Renaissance classicism and assembled at Hardwick a team of skilled designers, giving them an enormous budget and an imposing site to try out new ideas while retaining the elements essential to the building's practical and symbolic operation. Bess welcomed the fusion of tradition and innovation that made her new house a fashionable showplace where she became part of the spectacle. In this way, physical presence and architectural presence elide at Hardwick. Indeed, Bess's own initials, ES, decorate the high parapets, unambiguously marking the house as her property and personal creation. The country house took on a new form and meaning at Hardwick. And I wonder whether it can be simply coincidence that the first break with traditional planning in Britain occurs in a country house built for, and arguably also by, a woman. Hardwick allows me to introduce an important theme in this book: the role of women in the production of architecture and as architects.

Bess of Hardwick was only one of many women patron-builders active from the 16th to the 19th centuries. Accounts, diaries, and record books demonstrate the influence of women on the building, for example, of houses, schools, hospitals, and gardens. Lady Anne Clifford (1590–1676) oversaw the improvements to her Westmorland estates, including her castles at Appleby, Brougham, Brough, and Pendragon, as well as two new churches and alms houses at Appleby, and the erection of many monuments. The Grand Tour is usually seen as an essential part of a gentleman's education in European culture and included many sites of architectural interest. But it was also taken by women, and we find that after a Grand Tour lasting ten years the cousins Jane and Mary Parminter designed and built their house, A la Ronde (1792–8), whose distinctive, octagonal shape was based on San Vitale in Ravenna (Figure 3). The house comprised twenty rooms of which those on the ground floor, originally connected by sliding doors, radiated out from a 10.7 metres (35 feet) high central space, known as The Octagon. The spaces between the principal rooms were filled with triangular shaped closets with diamond shaped windows. Mary Parminter survived her cousin Jane, and her will specified only 'unmarried kinswomen' could inherit the property. And this remained the case for almost a century after her death. The Parminters were also responsible for a chapel and alms houses for unmarried women, and a girls' school. Women were active designers in other ways too. For example, the 2nd Duchess of Richmond and her daughters designed and decorated interiors and garden buildings of the Shell House at Goodwood (1739–46). Mary Townley, a cousin and pupil of Sir Joshua Reynolds, was arguably one of the first women architects. She designed Albion Place, a barracks, and several houses in Ramsgate. Her husband James was the principal investor in these schemes, which also included their own home, Townley House Mansion (1792).

These examples of women patron-builders are indicative of a more diverse approach to British architecture than we might find in some of the canonical histories that I have discussed. Of course, there are also many examples of male patron-builders and amateur architects in the period before the profession was formalized with the founding of the Institute of Architects in 1834, which later became the Royal Institute of British Architects (RIBA). Notably, women were not excluded from membership, but this was due to the fact that architecture was seen as a solely male preserve, so any such rule was not considered necessary. Like their male counterparts, women could become architects through the system of pupillage; however, the amateur status of women remained the case until the end of the 19th century. It was only in 1898 that Ethel Charles's application was accepted by a single vote after a debate in the RIBA council. She had been a pupil of the architect, Ernest George. Her sister Bessie was admitted in 1900, but both found their opportunities limited to small domestic works. Women began attending full-time architectural courses in around 1905 in Glasgow and 1909 in Manchester. Ironically, the Architectural Association, founded in 1847 with the intention of providing a more progressive way of training architects, did not admit women until 1917. Almost seventy years later, in 1985, the Women

3. A la Ronde, Devon (1792–8).

Architects Forum was established by RIBA, partly in response to the fact that fewer than 5 per cent of chartered architects were women. This was followed in 1993 by the Women Architects Group, renamed Women in Architecture in 1999, by which time 8 per cent of architects were women. A year later this group became independent of RIBA and set up the equality forum, Architects For Change, which included Women In Architecture, the Society of Black Architects, and the student forum Archaos.

Diversifying British architecture

My purpose in narrating this brief overview of examples of women's involvement with architecture is not to add women to the narratives of history that focus on the contribution of (usually male) individuals. Nor is to provide a potted history of known women practitioner/patrons. It is to show there are other ways of approaching historic British architecture that can make it a more diverse category despite its underlying class and gender assumptions. Here it is worth noting a recent analysis of the make-up of the architectural profession today. In 2019, a report for the Architects' Registration Board (ARB), the statutory body that prescribes architectural qualifications and maintains the Register of Architects, gathered statistics from the 43,000 registered architects. Data accounting for 100 per cent of members showed that 71 per cent of all of those on the register were male, but for the first time the gender split was exactly 50:50 for architects under the age of 30. Architecture still remains predominantly white; of the 62 per cent of architects who disclosed their ethnicity, only 1 per cent identified themselves as Black. This shocking statistic is in no way indicative of the richness that ethnic minority architects have brought to British architecture. Indeed, this short book would not be complete with the inclusion of star architects such as David Adjaye and Zaha Hadid. The RIBA Gold Medal for an outstanding contribution to international architecture was awarded to Adjaye in 2021 and Hadid in 2016, which, together with the appointment of Muyiwa Oki as president of RIBA in 2023–5, gives an important signal of much needed change. Indeed, Oki founded the Multi-Ethnic Group and Allies network to drive cultural change in the architectural profession. Notably also, Hadid was the first woman to receive the Pritzker Architecture Prize in 2004. And unlike many other women architects, who worked with their husbands, including Alison and Peter Smithson, Maxwell Fry and Jane Drew, Richard and Su Rogers, and Norman and Wendy Foster, Hadid ran her own highly successful practice.

We will come across the work of many ethnic minority architects in subsequent chapters. My question here is: how can we reconfigure histories of British architecture over a broad sweep of time to make these narratives relevant to a diverse range of publics? In answer to this, it is helpful to think about architecture, whether by a named designer or not, as having cultural value that can shift over time and mean different things to different publics. Moreover, architecture can embody intangible heritage—that is to say historical and cultural value that is not necessarily evident in the form or style of the building. It is the space where things happen that gives architecture its significance. Different communities may value different things, and again these may change over time. If we expand our purview beyond the established tropes of style, chronological sequence, and the primacy of the usually white male architect, we can understand British architecture in a much wider and inclusive context.

Architecture and cultural value

How then do we identify cultural value in a way that democratizes architecture? And what aspects of a building do we prioritize in determining 'value', which may shift over time and mean different things to different publics? Consider first the National Heritage List for England, or 'The List', and the circumstances behind it being established. My point here is not to give an extensive account of the evolution of this complex process, which inevitably continues to divide opinions about the restrictions placed on the re-use and redevelopment of buildings. It is more that The List shows us another way in which historic architecture in Britain is evaluated and recorded, and what it might mean to a diverse population. Importantly, in recent times the social and cultural value of a building is beginning to assume equal significance to its architectural style or authorship when assessing its merit. The first powers of protection for ancient monuments of national importance were established in 1882 with the First Ancient Monuments Protection Act (1882) which established a schedule of sixty-eight monuments in England, Wales, and Scotland. Almost all were prehistoric, including some of the most famous such sites in the country, such as Stonehenge. Subsequent amendments, in 1900 and 1913, allowed the inclusion of later monuments and introduced greater levels of protection and fines to prevent damage.

These developed into what we know today as statutory 'Listing' just after the Second World War. The listing of buildings of special architectural or historical interest was established in the Town and Country Planning Acts of 1944 and 1947. The basis for the first listing survey were the 'Salvage Lists'. These were drawn up to determine whether a particular building should be protected from demolition if bomb damaged. The fact that this became an activity of national importance during wartime tells us something of the significance attached to the built environment, and to architecture and buildings of various sorts as emblems of national identity. As The List grew, a system of grading and specific criteria was introduced to differentiate between the status of protected buildings, monuments, and sites.

The Ministry of Housing and Local Government conducted this pioneering survey comprising 120,000 entries. It took over twenty-five years to complete, and it mapped for the first time the built heritage of the country—we can think of it as a kind of 20th-century architectural Domesday Book. The entries were mostly medieval churches, country houses, and pre-1750 buildings. The information in these first list entries was quite basic, as they were often drawn up without the benefit of an internal inspection. The intensive urban redevelopment of the 1960s prompted a resurvey. The survey, carried out in 1968, focused first on thirty-nine historic cities and towns whose centres were particularly threatened by postwar redevelopment. This was followed in 1980 by a complete resurvey of the entire country. This resurvey extended the range of structures and building types recommended for listing, as well as the date range, to include more modern structures such as lidos, airports, cinemas, and smaller structures such as tombstones. But the system only protected buildings dating from before 1939. In 1987, the 1939 ceiling on listing buildings was lifted, replaced by the 'thirty-year rule' that operates today. Since then, the range of types of listed buildings has diversified to increasingly reflect a multicultural society. And as an indicator that values shift over time for everyone—many of the concrete modernist structures that were part of the rapid demolish and rebuild processes of the 1960s, which had prompted the resurvey in 1968, are now listed. Most importantly, the organic evolution of The List is indexical of how buildings may stay the same but their meaning to diverse publics can change over time. The changing cultural value and meaning of British architecture is a theme to which I will return throughout this book. But I would like to explore it briefly here by focusing on selected examples of faith architecture that serve a multicultural society.

A comparison between two mosques, both of which date from 1889, shows how the buildings can be valued in different ways. The Shah Jahan Mosque in Woking is the earliest purpose-built mosque in Britain, although initially it was for private rather than general use. It was commissioned by Dr Gottlieb Wilhelm Leitner (a Hungarian-Jewish linguist who had converted to Islam) and was partly funded by the Sultan Shah Jahan Begum, the female ruler of the Indian state of Bhopal. It was designed by a local architect, William Isaac Chambers, in a late Mughal style. The main façade is finished in white stucco and has four panelled piers crowned by green sphere finials and is surmounted by the dome, also in green. The main entrance comprises a full-height ogee arch and metal arabesque work with blue inlay to the arch spandrels. The building has Grade I listed status—according it the status of one of the most significant architectural examples in England.

By contrast, 8 Brougham Terrace in Liverpool is thought to be Britain's first fully-functioning mosque. Unlike the Shah Jahan Mosque it is located in an ordinary late Georgian terraced house dating from c.1830 that was bought by the Muslim convert William Henry Quilliam in 1889 as a base for the Liverpool Muslim Institute, founded in 1887. The building was originally listed at Grade II in

1985, partly based on it being a good example of an early-19th-century terraced house that retains much of its original architectural character. Both this type of speculatively built townhouse and the nature of the wealth of Liverpool (and many other cities) as an international port city in the Georgian period are themes that recur in later chapters. The original listing recognized the importance of the 'ordinariness' of the architecture of the building. However, in 2018 it was upgraded to II* in recognition of its intangible heritage: the space of the building is significant in telling the story of the emergence of Islam in England. Indeed, the 'house mosque'—a domestic dwelling converted to a place of worship—has become an important building type. For example, a mid-19th-century terraced house, 30 Howard Street, Bradford, was converted into a mosque in 1958 to serve Muslim migrants who worked in the textile industry. It is Grade II both to recognize and protect its intangible heritage and as it is a good example of Bradford's urban expansion when the textile industry made it one of the wealthiest cities in Europe in the 19th century.

The re-use of secular buildings for different faiths is not uncommon. One of the first Buddhist buildings was the London Buddhist Vihara in Chiswick, founded in 1926. It moved to its current location in 1994, occupying a community centre designed by the architect Richard Norman Shaw in 1877-8 for the residents of the up-market housing development of Bedford Park—for which it had been Grade II listed in 1970. Similarly, Christian buildings can also be repurposed. We see this for instance in the re-use and ongoing development of buildings as *gurdwara*s for Sikh communities. St Luke's Church at Cranbury Avenue, Southampton, a Grade II listed building, has traces of its previous use before it was bought and repurposed by the Singh Sabha. Similarly, the interior of the Ramgarhia Gurdwara on Chelsea Road, Bristol, provides clues to the fact that the building was once a church and then a leather goods factory. But in the case of many faith buildings, it is the religious practices which make the building a holy place. And the cultural value of the building for the community is clear. These building types continue to be adapted to the changing needs of their communities, while making a significant contribution to our built heritage. The original function of a building, especially one that already had listed status, is then one of the many values and meanings it held and/or holds within a locality. But we must not forget that apparently ordinary buildings that might not necessarily have architects are also important examples of British architecture.

And now to bicycle sheds

At the last count, around fifteen bicycle sheds merit the status of being a listed building in Britain. These have their own intrinsic diversity both in form and in the public they were designed to serve. Here I focus on two examples, both of which have named architects. The first is a brick-built bicycle shed designed by the Arts and Crafts architect, M. H. Baillie Scott as part of Waterlow Court, a Grade II* listed housing for women in Hampstead Garden Suburb (1908–9). The Arts and Crafts design of this new kind of structure is a picturesque architectural treatment based on the vernacular architecture of the past. And this is enhanced by the materials and detailing, such as the use of tiled roofs and a gabled porch clad in 'wany-edged' timber. There is also a contrastingly forward-looking element to this shed embedded in its cultural value: it signals how the bicycle, which afforded them more freedom, became increasingly popular with women at the turn of the 19th century. Indeed, the bicycle was very much part of modernity, and it transcended class, gender, and age divides. We see this in the bicycle sheds at Easington Colliery School that form part of the Manual Instruction Block designed by J. Morson of Durham (1911–13). They were identified as play sheds on the original plans, but were later used for bicycles. Their design could not be more distinct from those at Waterlow Court. Here a single-storey shed with an open front with iron columns facing the playground is a common arrangement for both types of building.

I want to end this brief consideration of bicycle sheds with a recent example by Sarah Wigglesworth Architects (2009). The Bermondsey Bicycle Store (Figure 4) is situated in the Bermondsey Square, a mixed-use regeneration area in South London. The site, formerly called the Court Yard, was originally the main quadrangle of an 11th-century Norman church, Bermondsey Abbey, which was mentioned in the Domesday Book. The landscape setting for a development on the site was inspired by the rich history of the area and the well-known Antiques Market. It was conceived as a carpet upon which are scattered an array of jewels—benches, bollards, cycle hoops, petanque pitch, and the bicycle store. The store houses seventy-six bicycles and is notable for its design, lighting effects, and use of materials. The enclosure is formed by thirteen Douglas Fir portal frames clad on the internal face with translucent glass reinforced plastic (GRP) sheeting to provide natural diffused light. As the light enters it is diffracted and flares on the nodal points of the external cladding panels. This external skin relates to the overall

4. Bermondsey Bicycle Store, London (2008).

design of the regeneration area. It comprises a series of scattered triangular stainless steel cladding panels, based on the geometry of several unravelled gem-like bollards from the landscaping. The interior of the bicycle store houses a clever double-stacked bike rack system by 'Josta' and includes sensor-integrated lighting—a bonus for its users. Returning to our starting point of Pevsner's dictum—how can we not see a bicycle shed as a work of architecture?

Lincoln Cathedral versus the bicycle shed

Our journey from Lincoln Cathedral to the bicycle shed has certainly provided us with the temporal parameters for the chapters that follow. More importantly it has introduced important themes that I will explore in more detail, as well as how they interrelate and the insights they offer into the rich and diverse nature of British architecture. We have seen how the questions of class, gender, and culture can be traced in the move from master mason to the gentleman architect, and eventually the formalization of architecture as a profession. The aim here is not to reinforce the idea of the architect as white and male; rather it is to open up the question of who can be considered an architect. We have seen the complexities of the processes of the design and the production of a building as part of an ongoing historical interaction rather than the preserve of more recent practice where architect and engineer stand as distinct from each other. I have also touched on the richness women and ethnic minority architects have brought to British architecture. And this has led to the notion of how we can rethink architecture and move away from canonical histories and narratives that focus on named architects and privileged patrons so that it becomes relevant to a diverse range of publics. And in doing this we see that architecture is not frozen in time: buildings can be remodelled and extended, their function and surroundings changed, and their histories written from various perspectives. 'Lincoln Cathedral versus bicycle shed' leaves us with a conundrum: what is the relationship between past and present in British architecture? I begin to tackle this enigmatic question in the next chapter.

Chapter 2
The love of the past

Revivals and nostalgia are arguably two of the most enduring themes in British architecture. This love of the past can make us want it to be a nice place. But the past is not static, it develops and changes according to the ways in which we engage with it. As such, the past and the nostalgia that might be expressed for it are mutable. The values that we recognize in the architecture of the past can, then, be viewed differently by subsequent generations as a broader range of publics engage with what we might call the built heritage. These expanding and more inclusive histories are crucial for a more comprehensive understanding of British architecture and what it means in a multicultural environment.

We saw in Chapter 1 how a preoccupation with the idea of the architect can influence how we write and think about architecture, and how these values can shift over time. In this chapter, I explore the love of the past in British architecture in parallel with the equally dominant theme in British architecture: style. The love of the past as manifest in architectural style shows that the aesthetic is not a constant value and our view of it may change over time and have different cultural meanings. But architecture is more than façades; it is a lived experience—a set of spaces which stage social and cultural relationships. And I would argue that the choice of aesthetic is only one element in this complex set of interactions that give the architecture of the past a volatility of meaning. My questions here focus on whose past we are discussing, and how its value to a range of publics shifts over time.

By exploring the relationship between style and architecture, I intend to examine how the use of past styles can widen our understanding of British architecture and what it means to a diverse public. Such an examination will also disrupt the comfortableness we sometimes feel about the architecture of the past to show that it also contains narratives that are extremely challenging to the present-day reader. Here, I am talking about the dominance of social elites and how they accumulated their wealth in a global context through colonization, slavery, and the slave trade, as well as the appropriation of wealth by looting. At home their fortunes were also augmented by radical changes to farming and land management systems, as well as by industrialization. These exploitative practices are embodied in the architecture that was commissioned and inhabited by the privileged few. We cannot ignore or erase this elite group from history; however, we can question and interrogate established hegemonies rather than accept them as the normative history. Indeed, we can, and in fact must, also seek out and tell other histories.

Let's begin with one of the most significant styles in British architecture—classical. By this, I mean the architecture of the Greco-Roman past, and how this enthusiasm for antiquity manifests itself in styles such as Palladian and neoclassical style, as well as subsequent variations of these design principles. This goes right to the heart of the relationship between the nostalgia for the past and the value system attributed to classical British architecture and, importantly, how these values differ across time. During the 18th century, such was the enthusiasm for the classical past that the image of whole cities was recast. Bath revived its ancient Roman roots, and we see this in the architecture and planning of designers such as John Wood the Elder. The nearby hot springs had been used by the Romans for bathing. This classical past was revived by Wood in his grand vision for the city. His plan included The Circus originally called King's Circus, as well as Queen's Square, and the Forum (which was not built). The classical influences are evident not only in the names but also in their Palladian design. It has been suggested however that The Circus (1754–69) (Figure 5) also references Britain's prehistoric past, as its diameter equals that of the nearby prehistoric monument of Stonehenge, which coincidentally Wood had surveyed. Indeed, the passion for the past went beyond the built environment. For instance, Edinburgh became known as the Athens of the North, in part for its classically inspired architecture as well as for its reputation as a centre for learning. A competition was held in 1766 to design a New Town or northern suburb linked to the Old Town by a new bridge. The aim was to develop a modern urban plan to promote the status of the city. In 1768, James Craig won the competition and his layout remains largely unaltered, with broad east–west avenues separating housing blocks bisected by smaller mews (Figure 6).

5. The Circus, Bath (detail) (1754–69).

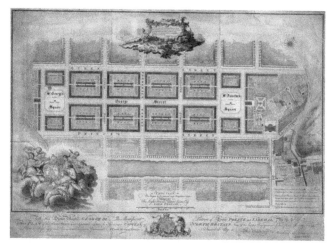

6. The First Plan of Edinburgh New Town (1768).

Classicism

The architecture of antiquity remains of fundamental
importance to our understanding of the practice of design, and
its relationship to culture and society in the West. How then do
we unpick its meaning in Britain? Why, in particular, would
classicism appeal when it is not an indigenous style, especially
at times of heightened nationalistic sentiment in Britain such as
during the period *c.*1680–1830, known as the long 18th century?
This enquiry may also provide some clues as to why classicism
became such a dominant narrative in so many histories of
British architecture. The move towards 'classical' formulae in
art, architecture, and literature gave British culture an
appropriate pedigree and intellectual basis. The nation's belief
in its cultural superiority over the rest of Europe meant it saw
itself as the inheritor of the mantle of ancient Rome. Indeed,
18th-century British society viewed itself as the Augustan era.
This self-conscious construction of culture makes a classical past

out of current beliefs and values. Classicism, in its broadest
sense, is used according to its utility in a contemporary
ideological system.

In this way the re-use of antiquity is an invented memory with an
ideological end. This helps define what the use of classical motifs
means in a broader historical context—for instance, the adoption
of building types unsuited to the British climate, such as the villa,
which was in effect more of an 18th-century fashion accessory
with a limited shelf life. Chiswick Villa is a good example. It was
designed by one of the leading architects of the early 18th
century, Richard Boyle, 3rd Earl of Burlington, who was greatly
influenced by the Italian Renaissance architect Andrea Palladio,
as an addition to his house on the outskirts of London. The villa
had no identifiable living accommodation, and was intended to
be a temple of the arts. Despite its competent celebration of
classical architecture, the bijou scale of the villa attracted much
attention, causing Lord Hervey, a contemporary commentator, to
remark that it was 'too small to inhabit, and too large to hang to
one's watch'. Equally, the increased knowledge of the architecture
of ancient Greece and Rome, and Renaissance Italy had a
substantial influence on British architecture of all types. We see
this in ecclesiastical buildings like St Paul's Cathedral (1675
onwards) and country houses such as Kedleston Hall (1765), as
well as in the form and layout of cities across the British Isles.

The questions that I would like to explore are: what did the
architecture of the Roman past offer 18th-century Britain? And
in which ways did it enable the projection of a national identity?
But first let's consider how architects and patrons learned about
classical architecture. Most obviously, increased travel led to
direct contact, but knowledge was also spread through the
contemporary burgeoning print culture. Architectural books,
patterns books, and treatises, many of which were translated
into English, meant that both the principles of classical
architecture and prime examples of it became widely available.

In Chapter 1, we encountered the early beginnings of the use of the architecture of antiquity in Hardwick Hall and other Elizabethan prodigy houses, which were influenced by Netherlandish, French, and Italian Renaissance classicism. We have also come across the most potent manifesto for classical architecture: Andrea Palladio's *I Quattro Libri dell'Architettura* or *Four Books of Architecture* (1570). The work comprises reconstructions of the architecture of the ancient Roman world with textual commentaries as well as representations of Palladio's own buildings. Palladio sought to revive the principles that had underpinned ancient architecture, including proportion, symmetry, and the correct use of the classical orders. Importantly, Palladio illustrated his text with elevations, plans, and sections of the architecture he discussed. Moreover, he pioneered new techniques of architectural drawing, including the use of orthogonal projection—a means of representing three dimensional buildings in two dimensions. In this way the proportions and measurements of a building were readily available and easily understood, even by a reader who did not speak Italian. Consequently, *The Four Books* was used across Europe as a guide to the architecture of antiquity as well as to Palladio's own buildings. Although it was not available in English until 1715, *The Four Books* rapidly became a crucial interlocutor between the architecture of antiquity and those with an antiquarian interest in the 17th and 18th centuries. One of Britain's first and perhaps best-known classical architects, Inigo Jones, used *The Four Books* as a source for his designs and as a guidebook for his travels in Italy. We still have the copy he used as his guide, which also includes his handwritten notes on the buildings that he visited in the margins of the pages. Perhaps in a first hint of how classical architecture was to become the 'national' style, Jones incorrectly identified Stonehenge as a Roman ruin and early example of classical architecture in Britain, rather than as a prehistoric site.

On his return to Britain, Jones introduced pure Palladian classicism in his designs for the Queen's House in Greenwich

(1616–35) and the Banqueting House on Whitehall (1622) (Figure 7). The latter was an addition to the Palace of Whitehall, which was the creation of King Henry VIII, who intended it to be the largest in Europe. The palace was destroyed by fire in 1698, and the Banqueting House is one of the few remaining components. The interior decoration of the Banqueting House celebrated the divine right of kings—ironically, the execution of Charles I took place on a scaffold erected outside. The upheavals of the Civil War and the Interregnum or Protectorate (1642–59) were in part responsible for the lack of uptake of Jones's pure Palladian architecture. By contrast, in the later 17th century, after the restoration of the monarchy in 1660, the theatricality of the Baroque style captured the nation's imagination. The Baroque had emerged in Italy in the late Renaissance period. Its rich ornamentation, bold masses, curvilinear forms, and powerful lines broke the rules of classical architecture. The short-lived emergence of English Baroque is evident in St Paul's Cathedral, London, by Sir Christopher Wren. It was also influential in the design of country houses such as Castle Howard, Seaton Delaval Hall, and Blenheim Palace,

7. **The Banqueting House, London (1622).**

designed by the Restoration playwright and architect, Sir John Vanbrugh. Blenheim was initially part-funded by Queen Anne as a reward to John Churchill, 1st Duke of Marlborough, for his military triumphs against the French and Bavarians, including at the Battle of Blenheim 1704. Vanbrugh was to create both a home and a monument to project the nation's identity and military prowess. As such, Blenheim is a rare example of the re-interpretation of classical architecture in the dramatic English Baroque style. The principal focus of my discussion of the adoption of classical models of architecture focuses on the country house in the Georgian Period. But first of all, I want to think about how classical architecture was encountered and how knowledge about it spread.

Encountering the past

It has been remarked more than once that the past is a foreign country. So how was this foreign architectural terrain explored, and what made it British? Classical Roman and Renaissance architecture remained an important inspiration for British architects, and in the early 18th century a revival of interest in travel, especially the Grand Tour, expanded their stylistic repertoire. The tour introduced young men and women to the sights and sites of Europe. The route comprised a core number of European cities, which later in the century extended to include Naples, Sicily, and Greece. But the eternal city was never forgotten or avoided, and the main purpose of the tour was to experience ancient Rome. Here the patrons of the future mixed with antiquarians and architects, and even academics. Indeed, by the middle of the 18th century, the Caffè degli Inglesi in Piazza di Spagna, Rome, had become the established meeting place for British tourists. Edward Gibbon, the author of the six-volume *The History of the Decline and Fall of the Roman Empire* (1776–88), remarked, 'according to the law of custom, and perhaps of reason, foreign travel completes the education of an English gentleman'. That said, tourism was not solely the preserve of the single male, as newly-weds, families, and single women from across Europe also undertook these extended journeys. Notable here amongst British women travellers are the Parminter sisters, Jane and Elizabeth, who travelled for several years, with their cousin Mary Parminter and their friend Miss Colville (we have already encountered Jane and Mary as the designers of A la Ronde). Lady Mary Wortley Montagu was also an extensive traveller and her letters give us an insight into the female touristic experience. Indeed, the title of Montagu's published letters refers to 'Sources That Have Been Inaccessible to Other Travellers'. Her initial focus was on her travels in the Ottoman Empire which was not then part of the Grand Tour's extended itinerary. But Montagu spent the last twenty years of her life (between 1741 and 1761) mostly in France and Italy. The letters themselves frequently draw attention to the fact that they present a different perspective, and, as Montagu asserts, her writings give a more accurate description than that provided by previous (male) travellers: 'You will perhaps be surpriz'd at an Account so different from what you have been entertain'd with by the common Voyage-writers who are very fond of speaking of what they don't know'.

Suffice to say, the Grand Tour was an excellent introduction to classical architecture, as itineraries usually included examples of Italian Renaissance, modern and ancient Rome, and later ancient Greek architecture. These direct encounters with antique and Renaissance architecture inspired patrons to recreate their experience on the return to Britain. Their engagement with the past was important and clearly created a lasting impression on many visitors to ancient sites. But how was knowledge about classical architecture amassed and how did it spread? Literary guides to the architecture of antiquity became increasingly available. Alongside textual descriptions from the ancient world, including Pliny's *Natural History* and Vitruvius' *Ten Books of Architecture*, many illustrated studies by Northern European and Italian scholars of the architecture of antiquity and of the Renaissance became accessible to a broad public. We have noted that Palladio's *The Four Books* first became available in English in a translation by Giacomo Leoni in 1715. Neither the quality of the text nor the images, which were woodcuts, proved satisfactory; but an improved English edition, published by Isaac Ware, appeared in 1738. As well as providing a valuable visual source, *The Four Books* influenced Colen Campbell's *Vitruvius Britannicus*, a multivolume work that mapped out the classical architecture of the British Isles. It was not an architectural treatise but an assemblage of images which created a new and important archive of British classicism—that is to say, the use of the repertory of classical forms in a variety of configurations. And it included the English Baroque of Wren and Vanbrugh. The opening statement by Campbell makes his purpose clear:

> The general esteem that travellers have for things foreign, is in nothing more conspicuous than with regard to building. We travel for the most part, at an Age more apt to be imposed upon us by the ignorance or partiality of others, than to judge truly of the merit of things by the strength of reason. It is owing to this mistake in education that so many of the British quality have so mean an opinion of what is performed in our own country; though perhaps in most we equal, and in some things we surpass our neighbours.

Volume I of *Vitruvius Britannicus* appeared in 1715, the same time as Giacomo Leoni's English translation of Palladio's *The Four Books*. This date is significant, as the Stuart monarchy ended with the death of Queen Anne in 1714, and the British crown passed to George of Hanover in order to ensure the continuity of the protestant monarchy. Notably, both volumes were dedicated to George I with a clear message: under the new royal house, Palladio's principles flourish once more.

The country house

The country house is one of the best-known building types to emerge in the 18th century. Arguably, it remains one of the most revered building types in Britain and is a key component of the heritage industry. But what kinds of values does it represent? And how have these changed over time? It was quite distinct from the Elizabethan prodigy houses, as it redefined the relationship between the land owner and those living on their estate. Since the Norman Conquest of 1066, the ownership of land in the form of a country estate had been a prerequisite form of wealth for most individuals and families with social and/or political ambition. Certainly, from medieval times at least, those who owned land had considerable influence over the fate of the country. And we have seen in Chapter 1 the ways in which this impacted on the development of housing types, which reflected the complex sets of social interactions that took place in these domestic settings. Patterns of land ownership changed and, from the mid-17th to the end of the 19th century, the general trend was towards increasingly larger parcels of land being held by a smaller number of families and individuals, as estates were consolidated through advantageous marriages. Known as 'old money' or inherited wealth, these landed gentry and nobility also exerted control over those elected to local parliamentary seats, until the electoral reforms of 1832. Country estates were also a nexus for social and cultural exchange and networking for the upper classes on both a local and a national basis. As a consequence, the long 18th century witnessed a country house building boom. These houses were distinct from their predecessors in that they had no defensive purpose, reflecting the peace and prosperity that the nation enjoyed at this time. But more importantly they represented a complete break with the medieval style of building, adopting instead the principles of classical design. As noted, the arrival of the Hanoverian monarchy in 1714 marked a major break with the past and inspired a new, fresh style of architecture.

Despite the architectural optimism prompted by the Hanoverian succession, the new royal house did not build very much, preferring instead to occupy existing residences, including Hampton Court and Kensington Palace. It is perhaps easy, then, to see the Georgian country house building boom of the long 18th century as a paradigm of British architectural production, at a time of great peace and prosperity. But the increased wealth of the aristocracy nobility and gentry that fuelled this enthusiasm for classical architecture tells another story that shows us how values and meaning in architecture can shift over time. One way of exploring this is to think about the building boom as an indicator of social mobility and a manifestation of new kinds of wealth based on a different set of social and cultural values.

Many histories of the country house promote the idea that the past is a nice place, and country houses are seen as epitomizing Britishness. But there are other ways of thinking about the country house that tell quite different and far more challenging histories. We need to reposition the country house as a global phenomenon that has relevance to the rest of the world and reflects Britain's connections worldwide. How then do we confront a past that is very different from the fictitious one embodied in the eulogizing narratives of the classically designed country house? In response to this question, I want to curate a mini-exhibition of a sample of country houses to explore the complex histories and shifting interpretations of this building type. Each example shows us the different sources of wealth that funded country houses and how the architecture of antiquity was used to project the identities of the patrons. I present my examples in chronological order but, as we will see, this does not imply any kind of progression. Indeed, the interconnections between the houses display both common and unique elements in the use of classical architecture to project individual and national identity.

There is no doubt that some members of the aristocracy were fabulously wealthy. Their fortunes were inherited and may have been augmented by investments or other interests in trade. Land was also another important producer of wealth and we will return to this in Chapter 3. Here, I would like to focus on the relationship between Britain's colonial expansion and the evolution of the country house. Of particular interest here is the relationship between the influx of money from West Indian plantations and asset stripping of India carried out by the East India Company (making it the richest institution in Europe), and the slave trade with both the Americas, the Caribbean, and East India. Britain's colonial and imperialist expansion is closely entwined with the country house building boom. Some country house owners were directly involved in these colonizing practices, while others profited through related industries, financing, and investments. The social elite were not the only ones to amass large fortunes through the subjugation of others. From the 16th century onwards, the merchant classes had expanded and enjoyed considerable financial success. Their substantially augmented wealth was principally derived from trade either with the Caribbean and the Americas or with India. As a consequence, they sought increasingly to consolidate their socio-economic status and political aspirations by acquiring country estates and marrying their children into the landed classes.

From the mid-18th century until the abolition of slavery in the 1830s, the absentee landlords of West Indian sugar plantations and their heirs invested and settled in country houses and estates in Britain. A similar story is told of the famed 'nabob' (a term used to describe those who had made a vast fortune), employees and merchants of the East India Company returning to Britain from India with their (often immense) portable wealth, such as precious gems or other treasure. Company men, who had effectively subjugated much of the Indian subcontinent in the name of the East India Company, invested in land and property on their return to Britain, much to the consternation of the landed gentry. While the *nabobs* were generally treated with suspicion or hostility, many of the West Indian plantation and slave owners were accepted more readily. Perhaps this is because wealth gained in the West Indies came from land ownership, which the British landed gentry understood, whereas the portable wealth brought back from India was seen as 'alien'.

Marrying for money

There were many mutually advantageous marriages between the 'old money' of the landed gentry and aristocracy, and the 'new money' derived from mercantile trade in the 17th and 18th centuries. My first exhibit, Clandon Park, Surrey, is an example of how such marriages facilitated the country house building boom, and gives us some indication of female agency in this process. The estate and Elizabethan house had been purchased in 1641 from Sir Richard Weston by Sir Richard Onslow, MP for Surrey. Many members of the Onslow family followed political careers; three of them were Speakers of the House of Commons. The house was built by Thomas Onslow, 2nd Lord Onslow, who was a favourite of both George I and George II. Onslow was the founder of a ship insurance company that dealt with slave ships. In addition, in 1708 he married the heiress Elizabeth Knight, whose fortune was estimated at the enormous sum of £70,000. Elizabeth Knight inherited her wealth from her uncle, Charles Knight (d. 1706), who had been a slave trader and plantation owner. Her inheritance also included a plantation called Whitehall in St Thomas-in-the-East, Jamaica, which was then passed down the generations of the Onslow family. In return, Knight's immense wealth enabled her to move from the social milieu of the City of London and of Jamaican merchants and planters by marrying into the world of the British nobility.

The marital home was intended to project Onslow's newly acquired wealth and Knight's newly purchased status. The design was commissioned from the Venetian architect Giacomo Leoni in 1713, but Clanden was not built until *c*.1725–31. As such its design is an example of the early adoption of Palladio, comprising a rectangular building in red brick with stone dressings, both of which were popular features of Palladianism in the early 18th century. The symmetry and classical articulation of the main entrance on the west side is also typical. This comprises two storeys plus an attic and basement, and has nine bays, of which the centre three are stone-faced and pedimented, and there are also stone quoins at the ends of the façade. Of particular note is the interior two-storey Marble Hall with two superimposed Corinthian orders, of which the upper register is smaller, to create the perspectival illusion of greater height. The arrangement of the five ground-floor rooms around the hall is reminiscent of Hardwick. Although Clanden was slightly old fashioned by the time of its completion, its Palladian style and luxurious interior conveyed a distinct message of wealth and status to contemporaries. Today the house speaks more of how the direct and indirect profits from slavery were channelled into an architectural legacy that contemporary audiences need to confront.

Buying status

My next exhibit illustrates how *nabob*s used their wealth to commission buildings with which to establish themselves in Britain. Until 1765, part of the East India Company's business also relied on labour through enslavement, and the company was actively involved in trafficking people from West and East Africa and transporting them to their holdings in India, Indonesia, and St Helena. Robert Clive, perhaps the most famous *nabob*, purchased Claremont with the tremendous wealth he had made in India. To cement his social standing, he built a new house intended to be his main residence and to display the treasures he had amassed. The first house on the Claremont estate was built in 1708 by Sir John Vanbrugh for his own use. In 1714, he sold the house to the wealthy Whig politician Thomas Pelham-Holles, Earl of Clare, who later became Duke of Newcastle and served twice as prime minister. On his death in 1768, the duke's widow sold the estate to Robert Clive. Although Vanbrugh's English Baroque design was by then little more than fifty years old, it was aesthetically and politically out of fashion. Clive decided to demolish the house and commissioned Lancelot 'Capability'

Brown, together with Henry Holland and John Soane, to build a new house on higher and drier ground. The style of the exterior was rather conventional, if not backward looking, in its close adherence to Palladianism. By contrast, the interiors owed much to the contemporary, more fashionable, neoclassical work of Robert Adam. Claremont was a fabulously expensive project. Clive is reputed to have spent over £100,000 on rebuilding the house and a complete remodelling of the landscaped grounds. However, he never lived there, as he died in 1774—the year the house was finished.

Roman revivals and rivals

My third example shows us how both the influence of the Grand Tour and rivalry between members of the social elite impacted on country house design. In the mid-18th century, Sir Nathaniel Curzon decided to rebuild the Elizabethan manor of Kedleston. In contrast to the *nabob*s and other nouveau riche, the Curzon family had a long and distinguished lineage, having come to Britain from Normandy at the time of William the Conqueror and having been at Kedleston since the 1150s. Curzon wished to build a show palace and venue for lavish events to rival nearby Chatsworth. The original manor house of Chatsworth had been altered and rebuilt in a piecemeal fashion *c.*1680–1707 by the 4th Earl (from 1694 Duke) of Devonshire using his own designs and those of a variety of architects and masons including William Talman and Thomas Archer. The imposing aesthetic of the new house, its collections and interiors, as well the social and political standing of the Devonshires all contributed to Chatsworth's status as a power house. How did Curzon set about challenging the status of Chatsworth?

Curzon's substantial wealth meant he could afford the fashionable but very expensive Robert Adam as his architect for his new house, Kedleston Hall (Figure 8). Curzon had acquired his taste for the architecture of antiquity when on his Grand Tour during

8. Kedleston Hall, Derbyshire, south front (1759).

which he first met Adam in Rome. Adam was originally commissioned to landscape the grounds in 1758 and then took over the whole project from Matthew Brettingham in 1759. As a vigorous self-promoter, Adam was always on the lookout for a wealthy client and he was delighted with his commission, remarking that '[Curzon] is a man resolved to spare no expence, with £10,000 a year, good tempered and having taste himself for the arts and a little for game'. Adam's lavish plans for the grounds included temples, bridges, seats, and cascades. As a consequence, except for the 12th-century All Saints Church, the medieval village of Kedleston was demolished in 1759 to make way for the new house and its extensive landscaped surrounds. The house was a temple to the arts and was intended to showcase the finest paintings, sculpture, and furniture. Kedleston fuses Palladian design with the increasingly fashionable taste for the neoclassical that makes broader references to antique Roman architecture. As such Kedleston reflects the taste of both patron and architect and their fascination with the classical world of the Roman Empire. How was this achieved? Once again, Palladio provided guidance.

The plan of a central rectangular block with quadrant colonnades and rectangular pavilions followed Palladio's unexecuted but published design for the Villa Mocenigo. The large central block was a mostly uninhabited, opulently decorated entertaining space, with the servants' quarters and service areas housed in the west wing. The main house was never meant to be a family home; instead, a private family residence was built in the east wing. Although constructed in red brick, the house is faced in ashlar and render to give the impression of a stone building more in line with antique architecture. It has a rusticated basement, *piano nobile* (principal floor), and attic storeys. The entrance front of the house is on the north side and has been described as the grandest Palladian façade in Britain. The main block is spread over eleven bays with a giant six-column or hexastyle Corinthian portico in the centre over a basement of five round arches.

The south front which faces the landscaped gardens comprises nine bays and a shallow dome, and the *piano nobile* is accessed via a distinctive double staircase with sharply curved flights. The imposing centre piece is derived from the Roman Arch of Constantine with four detached Corinthian columns standing close to the pilasters against the wall. Each column carries its own piece of entablature with statues above; and an attic bears the date 1765, when the house was completed, although the interiors were not finished until the 1780s. The choice of a triumphal arch for the garden façade of a country house might appear unusual. But the message was clear. Instead of honouring the military success of a Roman emperor, here the triumphal arch celebrates art and prosperity. Notably, the statues at the top of the arch represent theatre, dance, prudence, and hunting.

Kedleston can be seen as an essay in how the experience of the Grand Tour impacted on the design of the country house and its landscape. And I have concentrated on the stylistic elements for that reason. But we must not overlook where Curzon's wealth came from. Doubtless he too was a beneficiary of Britain's colonial expansions overseas. And his building project was in part assisted by an inheritance from his unmarried sister, Eleanor, who amassed her own fortune on the stock exchange, investing in companies that profited from the exploitation of others. Although not my focus here, it is important to note that the erasure of the medieval past with the demolition of the village of Kedleston was not a unique occurrence. I will return to both Eleanor Curzon and the changing face of the countryside in Chapter 3.

A base in Britain

As we have seen at Kedleston, the Grand Tour encouraged land owners to build. On his return from Europe, Patrick Home of Billie built Paxton House, Berwickshire, from 1758. The house was designed by John and James Adam, brothers of Robert Adam—all three were sons of Scotland's premier architect William Adam. The Adam brothers drew on Palladio's designs as well as from ancient Roman architecture, but the house was built in a pink sandstone, giving it a local distinctiveness. The main façade of Paxton is beautifully proportioned, with an impressive entrance portico supported on full columns, flanked by a pair of symmetrical wings for the kitchen and stables.

In 1773, Patrick Home inherited Wedderburn Castle, and sold Paxton to his cousin, Ninian Home, a prominent plantation owner in the West Indies whose fortune had been amassed through using slave labour. Although not a frequent visitor, he wanted a fashionable base in Britain. The shell of the house had been finished, but the interiors, comprising large, light rooms, were incomplete. Ninian's enormous wealth meant he could afford the services of Robert Adam and Thomas Chippendale—the neoclassical dream team—to finish the interiors of the house. Their designs adorned the ceilings, walls, chairs, and tables with decorative motifs borrowed from ancient Rome like medallions, urns, and swags. Ninian's prominence in the Caribbean continued to grow and in 1793 he became governor of Grenada on behalf of the British crown. However, in 1795, Fédon's Rebellion against British rule, which was inspired by the ideals of the French Revolution, led to the capture and execution of forty-nine prominent British settlers, including Ninian.

My mini-exhibition of Clandon, Claremont, Kedleston, and Paxton demonstrates different aspects of the country house in terms of function and use, and how classical architecture was used to project and augment the status of the owners. Their designs also show us how fashions in classical architecture changed quite rapidly during the course of the 18th century. At the same time, we see how the building boom was fuelled by wealth gained from colonialism and slavery. Moreover, Kedleston shows us how these houses also represent acts of oppression within Britain itself with the demolition of entire villages—a point to which I will return in Chapter 3. Perhaps most importantly, these houses are indexical of a point we discussed in Chapter 1: buildings' stories are not immutable. They tell different histories to and have distinct meanings for a diverse range of publics across time.

Other pasts, other loves

So far, I have concentrated on the use of classical architecture in the long 18th century and the changing ways in which it can be re-interpreted. But there have been other revivals of past architecture. Here I focus on the re-use of Gothic design to explore two very different themes in British architecture: otherness and the re-invention of an idealized past. Arguably, Gothic design in the long 18th century can be seen as part of the Gothic Revival that flourished in the 19th century under the guidance of A. N. W. Pugin, and we shall encounter this later in this chapter. However, it is frequently distinguished from the 19th-century movement with the spelling 'gothick', which betrays a less archaeological approach to design than its 19th-century descendant. My question here is: how was a style of architecture that was so remote in time, and known predominantly from extant ecclesiastical examples rather than from architectural treatises, absorbed into later British design? I begin with a consideration of Horace Walpole, 4th Earl of Orford's, Strawberry Hill (1749), and William Beckford's Fonthill Abbey (1796–1813). Both Beckford and Walpole were wealthy aesthetes and authors of dark, fantastical fiction that became immensely popular. In very different ways, both men might be described as Queer. As a counterpoint, I will also look at the 19th-century example of Anne Lister's Shibden Hall.

Strawberry Hill is usually referred to as a villa (Figure 9). Inspired by Pliny's descriptions of Roman villas and Palladio's villa designs, these became fashionable in the 18th century as small country retreats, often on the outskirts of a major city. As we have already noted, Chiswick Villa is a case in point. It was designed by Lord Burlington with input from his mother Juliana and was an appendage to the family house on the outskirts of London. Their town residence remained Burlington House on Piccadilly in London (now the Royal Academy) and the family seat was Londesborough in Yorkshire. Strawberry Hill tells a slightly different story. Walpole was an MP and son of the 'first' prime minister, Sir Robert Walpole, who had commissioned Colen Campbell, amongst others, to design the palatial, Palladian Houghton Hall in Norfolk (1722 onward). Horace was under familial and political pressure to establish a country seat. In May 1747, he took a lease on a small 17th-century house which he purchased the following year. Walpole believed, 'his residence ought, he thought, to possess some distinctive appellation; of a very different character...', and he adapted the earlier name of the house to Strawberry Hill. Walpole rebuilt the existing house in stages (1749, 1760, 1772, and 1776) to his own specifications, giving it a Gothic style, and gradually expanding the grounds to 46 acres (c.19 hectares). Strawberry Hill was the first house without any existing medieval fabric to be built in the Gothic style, based on actual historical examples. That said, the villa has a fantastical appearance that is reminiscent of a stage set, with its

9. Strawberry Hill, Twickenham (1749).

stuccoed battlements on the exterior, together with the medieval mouldings and cathedral-like features that extend into the interior, which is made from wood, plaster, and papier-mâché, and includes ornate crimson and gilded state apartments. In order to design Strawberry Hill, Walpole assembled a 'Committee of Taste', which included his close homosexual friend John Chute, who lived at The Vyne in Hampshire. Walpole recognized the distinctiveness of his villa, which was primarily intended to be a place to entertain a privileged same-sex circle, describing it as 'a little plaything house...the prettiest bauble you ever saw'.

Fonthill Abbey extends the relationship between Gothic and theatricality. The patron and co-designer, William Thomas Beckford (1760–1844), was a student of architect Sir William Chambers, as well as of James Wyatt, the architect of the project. Beckford was fabulously wealthy. At the age of 10 he had inherited £1 million in cash together with a substantial annual income, as well as his father, Alderman William Beckford's Palladian country house, built in the 1750s. Although Palladianism was being replaced by a broader interest in neoclassical design, Beckford senior had drawn inspiration from Walpole's Houghton as a model for his power house. Fonthill outshone Houghton with its opulence, and became known as Fonthill Splendens.

As the son of a wealthy English plantation owner, William Thomas Beckford had no title and was described as 'the richest commoner in England'. Beckford's notoriety increased as he was bisexual, and an unproven homosexual scandal in 1784 led to a period of exile in Switzerland with his wife Lady Margaret Gordon, who later died in childbirth. After her death, Beckford travelled extensively in France, Germany, Italy, Spain, and Portugal. His periods of residence in Portugal between 1793 and 1798 provided him the opportunity to visit the monasteries of Alcobaça and Batalha. On his return to Britain in the early 1790s, Beckford decided to have a Gothic cathedral built as a home on his Fonthill estate, which he had enclosed by a a 6 mile (c.10 kilometre) long wall. Work spanned the years 1796–1813, and was an extravagant and eccentric exercise in Georgian 'gothick'. The original Palladian house was slowly dismantled and then finally demolished in 1807. It was replaced by Fonthill Abbey—a cathedral-like structure based partly on examples Beckford had seen in Portugal. The design was hugely ambitious, with a 276 feet (84 metre) high tower that collapsed repeatedly, even while it was being built. Beckford lived in Fonthill Abbey until 1822, when he lost two of his Jamaican sugar plantations in a legal action. He was forced to sell the house and its contents for £330,000 to the arms dealer John Farquhar. In 1825 shortly after the sale the tower of Fonthill Abbey collapsed and was not rebuilt.

My final example is Shibden Hall in Yorkshire, which dates from c.1420, and its 19th-century owner, Anne Lister. Shibden had belonged to the wealthy Lister family, who were mill owners and cloth merchants, since the early 17th century. Anne Lister became sole owner of the hall in the 1820s and commissioned the York architect John Harper and landscape gardener Samuel Gray, in 1830, to make extensive improvements to the house and grounds. A Gothic tower was added to the building for use as a library and the major features of the park created, including terraced gardens, rock gardens, cascades, and a boating lake. Lister's attraction to women is evident in her diaries. It has been argued that some of the work at Shibden was influenced by similar 'picturesque' designs found at Plas Newydd in Wales, which she had visited. Plas Newydd was home to the Ladies of Llangollen, who shared a romantic friendship. As such, Lister's remodelling of Shibden has been seen as an example of subversive, Queer architecture, because her designs balanced the need for a respectable reputation among her neighbours with her need for private space.

It is tempting to see Walpole's work at Strawberry Hill and Beckford's at Fonthill as being driven by similar aims; the romantic use of Gothic architecture was to a large extent motivated by the desire to exceed paternal architectural example. The theatricality and whimsy of the Gothic, albeit historically accurate, replaced the more rigorous order, proportion, and rule of Palladian design. But whatever the motivation for the use of Gothic design, the examples of Strawberry Hill, Fonthill Abbey, and Shibden Hall also allow us to explore the idea of the relationship between sexuality and architecture. By no means am I suggesting that it is only Gothic architecture that connotes queerness. My point is rather to show that the style of a building can be subject to many interpretations.

As a kind of footnote to what the country house tells us about the love of the past, I want to draw your attention to the estate buildings, which are frequently ignored. Arguably, these designs were among the most original works of English neoclassical architects, who were able to experiment in a way that might have been less acceptable for their other commissions. Styles ranged from the gothick and the Chinese, for instance Holland's Chinese Dairy at Woburn (1792) and James Wyatt's Gothic Dairy at Belvoir (1810), to the more predictable Italianate and neoclassical styles. Robert Adam's designs for a gardener's house at Cullen House, Grampian (1775) borrows heavily from 16th-century Italian architecture. Indeed, the influence of the Grand Tour can be seen in the adoption of particular architectural motifs used in innovative designs that were equal to any being produced in Europe at this time. The distinctive semi-circular shape of the Diocletian or thermal windows of the ancient Roman bath complexes proved particularly popular in barn design, as seen in the austere façades of Capability Brown and Henry Holland's Cadland home farm, Hampshire (1777), for the Hon. Robert Drummond. Equally, Sir John Soane's brick barn at Malvern Hall Solihull 1798 is one of the most splendid examples of the revival of the baseless Doric order of columns.

The idealized past

The country house demonstrates the way in which we can idealize the past. There are also examples of moments when styles were revived as a conscious evocation of past values. The reasons behind individual revivals varied. Here, I concentrate on the Gothic Revival—a dominant force in British architecture of the 19th century. In distinction from its 18th-century forerunner, the Gothic Revival embodies an intricate set of social and cultural meanings, and it was adopted by both church and state as an expression of Britishness. The original medieval Gothic style on which it was based was seen as quintessentially British, despite its clear connections with France that we encountered in Chapter 1. But Gothic Revival architecture is also closely associated with Catholicism and a re-awakening of high church or Anglo-Catholicism. It became an important instrument in the attempt to re-invigorate the 'true' English church through architectural stylistic uniformity. Consequently, many medieval parish churches across the country were 'restored' to an imagined stylistic state that frequently destroyed their original early medieval features. New churches were also constructed in a Gothic Revival style, as part of the response either to the growth in Catholicism, especially following the Act of Catholic Emancipation in 1829, or to the resurgence of the high church or Anglican communion. Augustus Welby Northmore Pugin was a crucial advocate of the Gothic Revival. The enthusiasm for and knowledge of Gothic architecture was augmented by his two publications. The first was *Contrasts* (1836), a polemical book supporting the revival of Gothic as a means to return to the religion and social structures of the Middle Ages. Pugin's *The True Principles of Pointed or Christian Architecture* followed in 1841, which promoted Gothic or pointed architecture as being truly Christian and advocated the use of traditional methods of workmanship. Pugin's ecclesiastical designs were for both Anglican and Catholic communities and included St Chad's Cathedral and Erdington Abbey in Birmingham. The enthusiasm for the Gothic Revival continued long after Pugin's death. Examples can be found across the British Isles, including the distinctive Cathedral Church of Saint Mary the Virgin, commonly known as St Mary's Episcopal Cathedral in Edinburgh (1874–9), designed by George Gilbert Scott. Its soaring three spires dominate the skyline of both the Old Town and the New Town.

Outside the realm of religious architecture, the use of Gothic became more complex, and varied considerably in its faithfulness to both the ornamental style and the principles of construction of its medieval sources. We see this for instance in the cursory use of pointed window frames and touches of Gothic decoration which dress up an otherwise 19th-century building in terms of its ground plan and construction methods and materials. Perhaps one of the best-known examples is the Palace of Westminster. As we noted earlier, the original medieval palace built by Edward the Confessor was the residence of the monarch. In addition, parliament normally met in Westminster Hall, which was built by William II and still survives. In 1534, Henry VIII acquired York Place from Cardinal Thomas Wolsey and renamed it the Palace of Whitehall. Although it remained a royal palace, Westminster became the house of both parliaments. In 1834, most of the palace complex was destroyed by fire, including Sir John Soane's recent classical additions. A competition was held for the rebuilding of the Palace of Westminster in either the 'Gothic' or the 'Elizabethan' style to underscore the historical longevity of the building and its intrinsic role in the representation of Britishness. Charles Barry, one of the leading classical architects of the day, called on Pugin's expertise to produce the required stylistic dressing of the winning design. The plan met the functional needs of the new Houses of Parliament, while its aesthetic projected a distinct national identity that was embedded in the Gothic past.

It was not only churches and governmental buildings that received a Gothic make-over. Other medieval structures such as castles were upgraded and expanded. For example, Cardiff Castle (or Castell Caerdydd in Welsh) combines an 11th-century medieval castle built on a 3rd-century Roman fort with a Victorian Gothic Revival mansion (Figure 10). The building was renovated in the 18th century by John, 1st Marquess of Bute. He commissioned Capability Brown and Henry Holland, who demolished much of

10. Cardiff Castle, Cardiff (begun in 11th century).

the medieval structure to create a Georgian mansion in landscaped grounds. But it was the 3rd Marquess who employed William Burgess to transform the castle with an extensive remodelling scheme. Burgess's lavish designs were funded by the marquess's fabulous wealth, gained from the local coal industry. Burgess's achievements include a magnificent suite of interiors and exteriors that also referenced the rediscovered Roman remains. At its most romantic, Gothic was seen as a way of regenerating British culture and society, as the medieval past was seen as offering a counterpoint to the ills of the 19th century. Medieval methods of craftsmanship, including the use of local materials and the vernacular style, were seen as socially beneficial. The actuality of the social systems of the Middle Ages was eclipsed by an idyllic notion of the past that could be retrieved solely through the aesthetic. Later in the 19th century, William Morris based his Arts and Crafts style of design on these principles, and they are typified in the Red House (1865), designed by Philip Webb for Morris as a showcase for his belief in the rejection of mechanization in favour of the labour of the individual. The Red House was also Morris's home, and this fusion of the love of the vernacular past and its perceived power to improve is a theme that I will explore in Chapter 3.

Chapter 3
There's no place like home

The phrase 'there's no place like home' will be familiar to many of us. The words are taken from an early-19th-century popular song by John Howard Payne, but they are perhaps best known as the closing line of the 1939 film *The Wizard of Oz*. Payne's lyrics allude to a tradition of celebrating the idea of home, no matter how modest it may be. This sentiment began to find a voice in the late 1500s in Britain. We might see the contentious claim made in 1628 by Sir Edward Coke, 'For a man's house is his castle, and each man's home is his safest refuge', as an extension of this idea. This assertion was embellished in 1763 by the British prime minister—William Pitt, the 1st Earl of Chatham, also known as Pitt the Elder:

> The poorest man may in his cottage bid defiance to all the forces of the crown. It may be frail—its roof may shake—the wind may blow through it—the storm may enter—the rain may enter—but the King of England cannot enter.

Clearly a house of whatever type, be it grand or modest, was and is home to more than just men. Here, the provocative juxtaposition of a sentimental song, politics and common law, and a fantasy film adds nuance to possible interpretations of the idea that there is no place like 'home'. As a physical entity, a home is known in terms of its location, its design—which may range from cottage to castle—and the amenity it affords. But a home can also be defined in terms of the kinds of relationships people have, or would like to have, with others inside and outside of the home. In other words, it is the space that delineates the private sphere from the public one. And these relationships may challenge the gender assumptions of the male-dominated home. Following on from this, a home can project a specific British cultural identity, and we have already seen some evidence of this in the preceding chapter. In this way, the notion of home is constructed in the memory and imagination as much as it is found in the actuality of a building. In this chapter I explore how these different concepts inform our understanding of the idea of home in British architecture. Using examples from rural and urban environments drawn from housing from a wide range of social groups, we will explore how home is a place that impacts on British society alongside how it is as a place upon which society impacts.

First of all, it is important to think about the demography of Britain and how this has changed in terms of its social and cultural composition and location. From the Middle Ages onwards the volume of the population of the British Isles did not increase significantly, suffering more from periodic severe reduction due to plagues such as the Black Death 1348–9. The economy was mostly agrarian and as a consequence most people lived in rural environments. However, from the early 18th century onwards the population grew rapidly. By the mid-19th century, Britain had become the world's first urban, industrial society with more than half the population living in towns or cities. Alongside the substantial increase in the size and location of the populace from the 19th century, its demographic has also undergone significant changes in terms of social class and ethnic origin, as Britain attracted migrants from across the world. What effect did this movement and increase in the population have on British architecture?

The view from the window

We have already encountered the country house as an indicator of social status and considered the part that wealth amassed from Britain's colonial expansion played in its construction. These substantial buildings also impacted on their immediate surroundings as the taste in landscape design and in farming practices changed. The porosity between the country house and its landscape found expression in spaces such as the landscape room, devoted to notable pictures of Arcadian scenes. Here I would draw attention to a common architectural feature: the large windows through which country-house occupants could survey their surroundings. What did land owners see when they looked out through the window? Although landscape design is not the concern of this book, Kedleston has given us an indication of the substantial transformation made by the elite to the rural environment. The aesthetic was a driving force in the 'smoothing and levelling' of the private grounds that were viewed from the house. But what of the wider vista? How did the aesthetic come into play here and what was the impact on the concept of 'home'?

In the previous chapter we noted that during the long 18th century land ownership was consolidated. Alongside this there were significant changes made to how land was farmed and landscaped. The advancements in agricultural technology made farming into a business. The improvements in husbandry went some way to achieving the self-sufficiency necessary to meet the needs of a population that doubled during the 18th century. Encouraged by King George III, who acquired the nickname 'Farmer George', as well as agricultural theorists, land owners abandoned the medieval open field system and consolidated their land into larger parcels under the management of a single owner or farmer. The practice of enclosure continued well into the 19th century and was accompanied by the building of a new road network to provide a more rational, usable system of access between the country estates, towns, and cities. But these changes meant large numbers of the rural population became unemployed and consequently homeless; a move to the city was often the only option. This greatly increased the urban population that needed to be housed.

As farming practices changed so did the design of the buildings, including housing. I want to begin with the model farm buildings of the great improver-landlords in the period from *c*.1770 to *c*.1815. These include 'Coke of Norfolk' (the 1st Earl of Leicester), the 1st Marquess of Rockingham, the 5th and 6th Dukes of Bedford, the 3rd Earl of Egremont, and the 2nd Marquess of Stafford. The increase in the size of farms led to new buildings and layouts, and rational and utilitarian design principles were employed to ensure maximum efficiency. Well-designed buildings were essential for the improver landlords and new style farmers and this was recognized by agricultural theorists like Arthur Young. This aspect of the design of a country house estate was perhaps closest in terms of function to Palladio's designs for his villas and their working farms in the Veneto. The farmhouse was a 'gentleman's house' similar in size and appearance to the rectory. Typically, the farmhouses built by Samuel Wyatt for 'Coke of Norfolk' had a main part comprising six bedrooms and six dressing rooms, and living accommodation flanked by small pedimented wings, one containing the kitchen and the other the business room. The new challenges presented by these projects, and their prestige, attracted well-known architects. As noted in the previous chapter, the likes of Robert Adam, James and Samuel Wyatt, Henry Holland, and Sir John Soane all produced designs for model farms and estate buildings.

Model housing had appeared on country house estates when entire villages were demolished and resited as part of the improvement of the estate or grounds, and we have seen this at Kedleston. This could be done for purely aesthetic reasons. Alternatively, these changes were the result of rationalizing farming practices, leading to a logical regrouping of residential properties. Sometimes this kind of housing had philanthropic undertones and these new model villages were forerunners of the garden city and important early examples of purpose-built mass housing in a designed landscaped setting. The nostalgic styles used for these new-build houses provide another instance of the re-invention of an idealized past we first encountered in the preceding chapter. One of the earliest schemes was implemented at Castle Howard in 1699. Others were New Houghton in Norfolk (1729) and Milton Abbas, Dorset (c.1774–80) for the 1st Lord Milton. The motivation for Milton Abbas was purely aesthetic—the house being rebuilt by William Chambers c.1771–6 in the gothic style. At the same time Capability Brown improved the park. Part of this redesign included the workers' housing being demolished and moved away from view of the house. The new resited village was designed by Brown and Chambers. It comprised rows of semi-detached cottages, built using sham techniques to emulate local Cobb construction, lining gently curving streets. Nevertheless, despite specific instances of total or partial rehousing, large numbers of the rural population were displaced and had no housing or employment as a result of the changes to farming practices. The systematic rather than organic development of farm buildings and gentry houses also applied to the new villages that were built when whole communities were moved due to the demolition and resiting. This is important as the changes in housing type in the country, together with the need to house the ever-increasing number of urban dwellers, both rich and poor, led to a more methodical approach to house design than had previously been seen in Britain. And this was necessary to meet the new challenges presented by designing not only a home suitable for the city but also the urban environment in which it was located.

The shift in Britain's demographics was significant, with people moving from the countryside across the four nations to seek work in towns or cities. Many of these new urban dwellers were relatively young, and London was a particularly popular destination. The Georgian townhouse is a key part of this activity, as at the same time as the displacement of the rural poor the aristocratic families chose to spend more time in London in the newly built great estates in the West End. The building boom that met the housing needs of the elite also provided employment for the poor. Here they found apprenticeships to the capital's numerous tradesmen, many of whom were involved in the building trade, or employment as domestic servants to the dozens of aristocratic families. By the end of the 18th century, London's population had reached nearly one million people, which meant almost one in ten of the entire British population lived in the capital. Similarly, the industrial cities of northern England, such as Manchester and Leeds, also witnessed an influx of newcomers who found work in the new factories and textile mills that had begun to appear from the 1750s onwards.

My own front door

It is often said that the preference for having one's own front door at street level is essential to the concept of home in British architecture. Indeed, Elizabeth I decreed that in order to avoid the plague, each household should have its own front door and forbade the sharing of dwellings. We can trace the theme of 'my own front door' through a selection of housing types in Britain from the 18th century to the present day. My focus here is on the ways in which architecture and building technology combined to meet the need precipitated by unprecedented demographic change. We have already come across medieval and early modern manor houses in earlier chapters. Here, I want to think about the impact of the Great Fire of London in 1666 on housing design. The fire, which had destroyed almost all of the City of London, was followed by numerous building Acts regulating the materials and design of townhouses to make buildings less combustible and the city a safer place to live. These measures were consolidated in the 1774 Building Act, which alongside fire prevention aimed to curtail any slipshod construction, and avert disputes between adjoining owners of party walls. The Act also identified four different classes or rates of houses by size and grade of materials, with a first-rate house being the largest and most expensive (Figure 11). The parcel of land to be developed was usually owned by a member of the aristocracy who sold a lease to speculative developers who would build the houses and sell on the leases. The contract between land owner and developers stipulated the rate or rates of house or houses and the obligations of the developers for building any necessary infrastructure—for example the road. The system of future-proofing wealth was analogous to those found on the country estates of the elite. Just as gentleman farmers developed the yield from the land, and woodland was planted for supplies in time to come, so the urban estates were made profitable at little cost to the land owner, who received ground

11. Examples of first-, second-, and fourth-rate houses.

rent and sold new leases for the houses once the term of the original ones expired.

The Acts, through the introduction of different rates of houses, enabled the identification of housing stock for different social classes and the decisions made by the landlord had a distinct impact on the demography of an area and patterns of population and class across London. This made zoning possible, as the building of houses of a certain rate would, in theory, ensure a certain class of occupier. Commensurate with this was the association of the different rates of houses with various classes of occupants as first-rate houses commanded higher rents than those of a lower rating. This identification is not foolproof—larger houses could provide lodgings for several families and the desirability of areas could change. But the rate system did facilitate the creation of areas with distinctive social aspirations. A first-rate house occupied an area of more than 900 square feet (84 square metres) and was typically for the nobility or gentry. These grand townhouses were often ranged around a garden square to which only the residents had access. A second-rate house, with a ground plan of 500–900 square feet (46–84 square metres), was for professionals such as doctors or merchants. Third- and fourth-rate houses were substantially smaller, with ground plans of 350–500 square feet (33–46 square metres), and housed clerks and artisans respectively. Importantly, each dwelling of whatever rate had its own front door. And this has remained a dominant trait in housing across Britain. Alongside the dimensions, the types of materials were also stipulated and to enforce the new rules, the statutory role of surveyor was established to ensure the correct construction of any new building.

In Chapter 1 we encountered the differentiation made by some historians between vernacular and polite architecture. My question here is what happened to the architect and the practice of architecture in the face of such an intense, regulated, urban building boom? Standardization and basic quantity surveying were the hallmarks of the production of the Georgian terraced house by a range of craftsmen. Once again, print culture was an important catalyst for changes in building practice but here the impact was more on vernacular architecture. The new regulations precipitated the rise of builders' books aimed at the various trades involved in the construction of this type of housing, for example William Pain's *The Practical Builder* (1774) was a comprehensive guide for carpenters, and later on, Peter Nicholson's *The New Practical Builder and Workman's Companion* (1823) was aimed at architects and the various building trades. In contrast to the architectural treatises of Palladio and other theorists, these books were more practical hands-on guides providing patterns for the design and layout of houses together with the various quantities of material—wood, brick, and so forth—necessary for their construction. This system of estate development is akin to a present-day design-build, where a contractor rather than an architect produces the design and carries out the construction of the outer building and the basic interior—a practice known as completing to shell and core. And this method of building also brings us back full circle to the master builders or masons we encountered earlier in this book.

Grosvenor Square, built between about 1725 and 1731, is a useful example of how estate development worked in the production of housing (Figure 12). The land was owned by Sir Richard Grosvenor, who subcontracted the work to build fifty-one houses to around thirty individual builders or partnerships of craftsmen. Houses were built to shell and core and the lease sold to the incoming occupant, who decided on interior finishes. The first residents were all from the upper echelons of society, including, for example, sixteen peers, mostly from the upper ranks. Notably, eleven of the houses were occupied by dowagers or unmarried women. These included Eleanor Curzon, the sister of Nathaniel Curzon who built Kedleston, both of whom we encountered in Chapter 2. Eleanor was unmarried and therefore able to control her own finances. Her independent London home was funded by

British Architecture

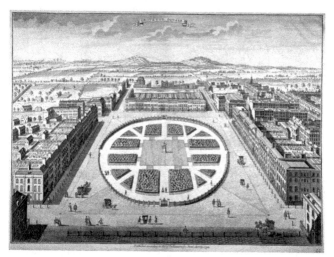

12. Grosvenor Square, London (1725–31).

Eleanor's substantial wealth, which was gained partly through inheritance and partly through her activities as a successful investor in public stocks and securities that benefited from Britain's colonial expansion.

The 1774 Act was initially aimed at London. But the standardization introduced by the Act, as codified in builders' books, meant that this method of design and build was soon taken up across Britain as the population of towns and cities increased significantly. Consequently, the Georgian terrace is a prominent feature of many urban environments, where whole streets and even neighbourhoods consist of the same size of house built in the same materials with very little ornament. There were regional variations; for example, in Edinburgh, the New Town was constructed mostly from stone, and in Dublin the houses were generally larger and the roads wider than their London counterparts. The enhanced materials and enlarged scale of these capital cities gave a sense of grandeur that is perhaps lacking in other examples of the Georgian terrace. The system of rating houses was also used as a model for the development of pleasure cities such as the spa towns of Buxton and Royal Leamington Spa, as well as Bath, which we encountered in the previous chapter. The ease with which urban environments could be built using the specifications for the Georgian townhouse also facilitated the development of port cities. The ending of the Royal African Company's monopoly in 1697 had enabled companies and merchants from the ports in Bristol and Liverpool to participate legally in the slave trade. Consequently, Bristol became the principal slaving hub, but by the middle of the 18th century it was superseded by Liverpool.

There was a rather different kind of urban development in Glasgow, which, after the Act of Union in 1707, could also participate legally in the slave trade. The city had initially grown wealthy on the tobacco trade, followed by imports of sugar and cotton which were produced by slave labour in the Americas and Caribbean. In the early 18th century, substantial Palladian-style detached mansions were built for the untitled but so-called 'tobacco lords' within the confines of the city. The Cunninghame Mansion is an interesting example of this building type and how the uses and meaning of architecture can change over time, as it now houses Glasgow's Gallery of Modern Art (GoMA). The small but impressive mansion was begun in 1777 for the tobacco and sugar merchant William Cunninghame of Lainshaw on a plot of land on Queen Street which was once agricultural ground on the periphery of Glasgow's western frontier (Figure 13).

From around 1750 a new urban plan emerged with which James and Robert Adam were among the leading designers involved. The plan included new streets terminating in civic buildings situated on an axis with many of the names having direct or associational connections to the slave trade. For example, Buchanan Street was named after the tobacco lord Andrew Buchanan, and Jamaica Street, Tobago Street, and the Kingston Bridge speak for

13. The Cunninghame Mansion now the Gallery of Modern Art, Glasgow (begun 1777).

themselves. The layout was influenced by examples from continental Europe, especially the housing, which mostly comprised large flats above arcaded urban premises. Tenements or blocks of flats with shared entranceways and hallways accessing individual flats were common in Scotland, but did not prove popular elsewhere in Britain until much later. A notable exception is John Nash's early-19th-century design for Regent Street in London. Here a portion of the street had colonnades to shelter pedestrians whilst they visited the shops at ground level. The flat roofs of these colonnades were also verandas for the well-to-do single men who occupied the apartments above when visiting town.

The invention of tradition

The influx of people into towns and cities certainly provided a workforce for the Industrial Revolution. But the rapidly increasing number of urban dwellers could not be housed. This resulted in overcrowding and poor living conditions which prompted the social reformer Robert Owen to address the problem. Owen established one of the first model communities in 1817 to house workers at his textile mills in New Lanark. He introduced social and welfare programmes implemented through the urban plan of the town. This kind of philanthropy was the prompt for a number of model villages built by 19th-century industrialists.

One of the first was Saltaire (1853–63) built by Sir Titus Salt, a leading industrialist in the Yorkshire woollen industry. Salt used the local architects Henry Francis Lockwood and William Mawson, who produced a rational grid layout of terraces, graded to reflect the status of the occupier, with a mill that resembled a Renaissance palazzo. In common with the improver landlords, these changes were driven by a wish for efficiency, to increase productivity. Later examples include William Lever, later Lord Leverhulme, who resited his soap factory to a location on the Wirral: Port Sunlight. He personally supervised the planning of the village, and employed William Owen and his son Segar as principal architects. Between 1899 and 1914, 800 houses were built, to house a population of 3,500 (Figure 14). The ideals of this kind of model village resulted in a style of architecture that drew on vernacular and Arts and Crafts elements to present a romanticized version of working-class housing. Bournville is a typical example of this kind of architecture. John Cadbury, a Quaker, began to sell tea, coffee, and drinking chocolate from his premises in Birmingham in 1824. The Cadbury family took a paternalistic approach to their employees on home soil. This is in contrast to the slave labour used in the production of their prime ingredients: cocoa and sugar in the Americas, Caribbean, and West Africa. In 1879 his sons Richard and George moved the factory to a greenfield site now known as Bournville. George Cadbury was appalled by the working-class living conditions in Britain and wanted to provide decent housing for his workers alongside the new factory. He planned a model village of well-built cottages with large gardens. The village would also have spaces for recreation and leisure. In 1895 more land was

Two Pioneer 'Garden Cities.
1, 2, 3, 4. Views in Bournville. 5, 6, 7. Views in Port Sunlight.

14. Bournville (begun 1879) and Port Sunlight (1899–1914).

purchased, and the architect William Alexander Harvey was
instructed that each house was to occupy no more than a quarter
of its building plot, and have a garden large enough for
cultivation. By 1905 315 houses were built. In 1906 a Workers'

Housing Co-Operative called Bournville Tenants Limited leased building land and added another 398 houses. The houses drew on a vernacular style of architecture, including Tudor-esque beams and overhanging eaves to give the feeling of the past. The traditional design of the exteriors, with their echoes of Arts and Crafts architecture, contrasted with their modern interiors. In 1913 a model garden suburb for white-collar workers was added. These designs became a blueprint for many other model village estates around Britain. The 1920s and 1930s saw rapid expansion of the land by various cooperatives and societies and private arrangements. The Bournville Trust remains active to the present day, providing social housing and community facilities.

The philanthropic approach to housing enjoyed less initial success in the private sector. In 1898, Ebenezer Howard published *To-morrow: A Peaceful Path to Real Reform* (re-issued in 1902 as *Garden Cities of To-morrow*). In response to the overcrowding and deterioration of cities in Britain, Howard's idealized garden city would house 32,000 people on a site of 9,000 acres (3,600 hectares). It was to be self-sufficient, with housing, communal building, and allotments planned on a concentric pattern with open spaces, public parks, and six radial boulevards. To attract private investors, he founded the Garden City Association, which created First Garden City, Ltd. in 1899. In 1904 the architects and town planners Raymond Unwin and Barry Parker won the competition to plan the garden city of Letchworth, situated 55 kilometres (34 miles) outside of London. The design of Letchworth is similar to the model villages but with perhaps more emphasis on Arts and Crafts detailing, with pebble dashed or painted roughcast walls for modest dwellings, red brick for larger houses and public buildings, and tiled roofs. Unwin went so far as to draft building regulations that included rules encouraging 'simple and straightforward building; the use of good harmonious materials', and discouraging 'useless ornamentation'.

Much of Howard's idealism in the planning of the Garden City and the types of ownership of the housing had to be compromised. As a consequence, Letchworth was not affordable for blue-collar workers, attracting instead mostly skilled middle-class workers. In 1920, using the same financial model, Howard developed his ideas with the construction of Welwyn Garden City. Howard had called for the creation of planned towns that were to combine the benefits of the city and the countryside and to avoid the disadvantages of both. Notably, the architectural style is distinct from other 19th-century examples and brings us back to the 18th century as the buildings are neo-Georgian. The town is laid out along tree-lined boulevards with a mile-long central mall—the Parkway. The interwar period also saw much local authority housing, some of which was based on garden city principles. The most comprehensive example is Wythenshawe, a satellite of Manchester separated by a stretch of greenbelt—a planning tool used to halt urban sprawl by placing a no-build 'ring' around a city. In 1931, working with the City Council, Barry Parker produced a plan drawing on garden city principles and American ideas of landscaped parkways providing high speed arteries through the city. The cottage-style housing was mostly of redbrick or had rendered walls with mansard roofs and is quite distinct from other examples of local authority housing, which were built on a tighter budget.

The urban disease

The endeavours of 19th- and early-20th-century philanthropists and idealists did little to combat the 'urban disease'. The Industrial Revolution prompted a vicious cycle whereby industry chose to set up near population bases to ensure labour demands could be met. In turn rural migrants seeking work moved into the city, placing increased demands on the available housing, but also prompting further industry. This resulted in greater pollution in the city, higher populations, and denser living conditions. But the model village and garden city found a reprise in the aftermath of the urban destruction wrought by World War II. The New Towns Act 1946, together with the Town and Country Planning Act 1947, created a revolutionary process of constructing new and fully planned towns that would decongest larger industrialized cities and halt the growth of London. In the latter half of the 20th century New Towns were built across Britain; each was intended to house around 60,000 people. These included satellites to London such as two of the first New Towns: Stevenage and Harlow. Elsewhere in England, Wales, and Scotland, these towns met local needs and were intended to address the poor housing conditions of those living in nearby towns and villages. Examples include Newton Aycliffe, Skelmersdale, Telford, East Kilbride, Glenrothes, Cumbernauld, Livingston, and Irvine.

A common theme in the regional New Towns is the development of the coal mining industry. Glenrothes was planned in the late 1940s. As one of the first New Towns in Scotland, it was intended to house miners who were to work at a newly established coal mine, the Rothes Colliery. Similarly, Cwmbran was designated as a New Town in 1949 to provide new employment opportunities in the south-eastern portion of the South Wales Coalfield. Peterlee, named after the celebrated Durham miners' leader Peter Lee, tells a slightly different story to other post-war New Towns. It was requested by local people, who were mostly miners, to combat the squalor of their living conditions. Despite the modest beginning and restricted budget, two of the best-known figures in 20th-century art and architecture were involved with the project. In 1947 the internationally renowned modernist architect Berthold Lubetkin was commissioned to be master planner and chief architect for the New Town, and he worked with the leading town planner Dr Monica Felton, chairman of the Peterlee Development Corporation. Lubetkin's masterplan included a number of high rise towers. But coal extraction was to continue under the site, which posed a risk of subsidence, so the National Coal Board (NCB) would only consider a dispersed low density development. No compromise could be found and Lubetkin resigned from the project in spring 1950. His only intervention in the scheme is in the opposed parabola forms of the road layout. In 1955 the abstract artist Victor Pasmore was appointed as the Consulting Director of Architectural Design for Peterlee. He chose to design the town around a central abstract artwork and pavilion that initially provided a pedestrian link between the two halves of the estate. Pasmore named it the Apollo Pavilion, as a reference to the optimism of the Apollo Space Programme. The bold geometric form in cast white concrete is an experiment in the synthesis of art and architecture. Pasmore described it as 'an architecture and sculpture of purely abstract form through which to walk, in which to linger and on which to play, a free and anonymous monument which, because of its independence, can lift the activity and psychology of an urban housing community on to a universal plane'.

Mutable spaces

Traditional or vernacular housing forms reveal patterns of habitation and these can change over time even though the building remains largely the same. Perhaps more complex is what the density of dwellings both in terms of occupancy and their proximity to each other reveals about the relationship between housing and social class. Here multigenerational households and multiple occupancy tell different stories of how architecture accommodated patterns of living across centuries and social divides.

In Chapter 1 I pointed out that architecture is mutable—its function and meaning can change over time. This idea is important for our understanding of the notion of home. To explore this in more detail, I want to return to the Georgian townhouse—the architectural 'response' to the coincidental increase in both population and urban living. My example is Fournier Street, which runs east from Nicholas Hawksmoor's Christ Church, Spitalfields (1714–29), in London. Alongside the constantly changing demographic of an ordinary house or street, Fournier Street, originally called Church Street, also shows us the slippage between polite and vernacular architecture. As a result of the Great Fire of London 1666, a commission was established in 1711 to build fifty new city churches. We must not overlook what a substantial challenge this presented to architects and commissioners in terms of urban regeneration in response to shifting demographics, and Christ Church, Spitalfields, was no exception. The Commission had acquired the site of 1 square mile (2.6 square kilometres) in the medieval parish of Stepney. It had been home to the Huguenots, Protestant refugees fleeing from persecution in Catholic France, around 50,000 of whom had arrived in the late 1680s. The project was in part intended as a show of Anglican authority to the Huguenots, who owed no allegiance to the Church of England and thus to the king. Alongside the church, Hawksmoor also designed the adjacent minister's house. The same team of craftsmen worked on the church and this highly specified design, including the carpenter, Samuel Worrall. Worrall took up the leases on several plots on Fournier Street as a speculative development and built houses using the same teams that had worked on the ecclesiastical buildings. Many of these houses were built for the wealthier Huguenots, who were master silk weavers and mercers. The houses are distinctive for the quality of their interior fittings, fine wooden panelling, and elaborate joinery, such as carved staircases and fireplaces. Equally important is the bespoke nature of their designs, to accommodate both the silk weaving on the well-lit uppermost floors and the layout of the ground floor rooms, which were often showrooms for the finished products.

By the early 19th century London's silk weaving industry was in decline and the Huguenot weavers moved on. They were replaced by an increasing number of Jewish *émigrés*, arriving in the 1880s to escape persecution in Eastern Europe and Russia, who joined the small community that had been established in the area for some time. The houses were part of a new thriving community including new schools, synagogues, and cultural centres. In the mid-20th century the houses changed again and became the residences of a large *émigré* Bengali community. Perhaps the most obvious barometer of the shifting demographics of Fournier Street and the mutability of architecture is the Huguenot Chapel ('La Neuve Eglise') constructed in 1743–4 at its easternmost end. This briefly became a Methodist chapel and in 1898 was converted into the Maz'ik Adath Synagogue, and became, during the 1970s, the London Jamme Masjid (Great Mosque). Today, the houses on the street have been largely bought and restored by the well-to-do as *bijou* Georgian townhouses whose exteriors and interiors remain largely unchanged from the early-18th-century originals. If only walls could speak.

Design for living

Today we see the kitchen as the hub of the home—but was this always the case? Let's go back in time and trace the location and use of this crucial domestic space, beginning with the tower house, which is almost indistinguishable from the medieval castle. Tower houses were constructed in Great Britain, particularly in Scotland, and throughout the island of Ireland, from the Middle Ages, until at least the 17th century. Examples in Scotland are most numerous in the Scottish Borders, where they include peel towers and bastle houses. Welsh tower houses were fortified stone houses that were built between the early 14th and 15th centuries. Tower houses have a compact footprint and as the name suggests comprise several storeys, each a single hall space with a specific function where servants and the elite lived under the same roof. Food was prepared in these areas and cooked on the open fires that also supplied heating. Communal living continued in the form of the medieval hall and endured into Elizabethan times, as we have seen at Hardwick, albeit with spaces designated for the various social classes.

The design of country houses and upmarket townhouses from the 18th century onwards marked a distinct move away from shared accommodation. Instead, servants became invisible—they had separate entrances and living quarters and circulated through the house using different staircases and access points to the principal rooms. In country houses it was not unusual to situate the kitchens in a separate wing or part of the building quite far away from the principal rooms to avoid the smell and the risk of fire. Sometimes these were connected to the main house via tunnels, such as those added to Uppark. Here, throughout the 19th century, food prepared in the kitchen was wheeled through subterranean passages on trolleys on its way to the servery, and servants could pass between the house and the service blocks without being seen. The invention of the range or stove, rather than cooking on an open fire, made kitchens in larger townhouses more practical—they were situated in the basement. In lower rate houses cooking such as it was continued to take place on the trivets which were an integral part of the fire grate. Kitchens only moved upstairs to the main living level of the house towards the end of the 19th century. Richard Norman Shaw's designs for Bedford Park—a kind of garden suburb on the then outskirts of London—is an early example. Shaw designed the kitchens to be small but on the main living floor. He wished to push the middle-class occupants into the other living spaces of the house. By the 1930s modular kitchen cabinets and continuous countertops and the invention of appliances radically changed the kitchen into a space where design and efficiency went hand in hand. This was typical of the principles of modernist housing design where the imposition of 'expert' knowhow impacted on the way people should live.

The public and private sphere

The social engineering of Bedford Park leads us back to some of my opening remarks about the notion of home and the green space that surrounds it in relation to the public and private sphere. The town and country houses of the elite played out these contrasting concepts by restricting access to certain spaces. We have already seen how the circulation of servants was controlled through certain parts of the interior. Alongside this the social rank of visitors determined which rooms they were received in. Similarly, visitor access to the grounds and expensively remodelled landscaped gardens that surrounded country houses followed the same rules of sociability and privacy. The garden square provided a hybrid space—only residents of the surrounding townhouses could enter but it was a shared area. Model villages and garden suburbs also aimed to reconcile the wish for privacy whilst producing environments that encouraged a sense of neighbourhood. These are typified by the importance of single dwellings with their own front door and a garden, and the communal facilities. The use of an invented architectural style presented the 'myth of merry England' through the use of idealized vernacular forms. But can the conflicting aims of privacy and sociability be met by a different architectural style?

To explore this question, let's consider two contrasting examples of modernist architecture, to show how house design can interact with the needs of its occupants for privacy on a range of levels. Gerald Schlesinger and his partner Christopher Tunnard commissioned the architect Raymond McGrath to design St Ann's Court, Surrey, in 1937. McGrath produced a three-storey circular modernist house cast *in situ* from reinforced concrete. The cylindrical structure took full advantage of the properties of the concrete as segments were omitted on various levels to provide terraces and balconies. Tunnard was a landscape architect and he worked as consultant on the house as well as redesigning the landscape. The innovative design of St Ann's Court was also a response to contemporary homophobia, when such a relationship could lead to imprisonment. To protect the privacy of the occupants, the master bedroom could be separated by retractable

There's no place like home

screens into two halves and the double bed also divided in two. In this way, the space could be transformed into two single bedrooms separated by a dressing room.

My second example is Harlow New Town—a result of the 1946 New Towns Act—and in particular the development of Area 71 of the overall plan, now known as Bishopsfield (Figure 15). In 1960 Harlow Development Corporation organized an open competition for the design of this neighbourhood, with the brief to provide a pattern of living better suited to the needs of modern urban society. The guidelines also stated that 'consideration should be given to the problem of providing privacy to the rear of the house and garden'. The competition was won by Michael Neylan, who had been working at the modernist architectural practice Chamberlin, Powell and Bonn—designers of the Golden Lane council housing estate in London. Nylan teamed up with Bill Ungless to design Bishopsfield (1961–6) comprising 267 dwellings, ranging from bedsits to houses with five bedrooms which were externally almost indistinguishable, arranged in a horseshoe around a central piazza. The site was on a slight hill and the overall plan was intended to resemble a hill-top village. The exterior and interior design of the dwellings, many of which were let furnished, combined the unadorned simplicity of the modernist aesthetic. Of particular note are the houses that became known as patio-houses due to their L-shaped plan ranged around an enclosed courtyard or garden, so affording the privacy rarely found in other estate developments where exterior spaces ran parallel to each other and were overlooked. Provision for a common room, shops, and a village green was intended to counter the emphasis on domestic privacy and foster a sense of community. But these plans were not implemented by the Harlow Development Corporation. Nevertheless, Bishopsfield enjoyed worldwide acclaim, which greatly enhanced the international significance of Britain's New Towns initiative.

15. Bishopsfield, Harlow New Town (1961–6).

Street life

The urban population of Britain increased ten-fold during the 19th century. Despite the inevitable squeeze on space, the single-family dwelling remained the preferred residence for anyone who could afford it. A flat had connotations of the socially inferior status of tradesmen. Neither was an option to the urban poor, who rented single rooms for a whole family in overcrowded properties. The street was crucial to all these types of urban dwelling. It facilitated circulation through the city, was a place for trade of various kinds, and enabled social interaction. Perhaps most importantly for the upper echelons of society the street provided a space between the private sphere of the home and the public sphere of the metropolis. What happens when a street is removed?

Towards the end of the 19th century a townhouse was becoming increasingly expensive to maintain, especially in London. The suburbs were one solution and we have already seen how developments like Bedford Park responded to the need for middle-class housing, with access to London facilitated by improvements in the suburban public transport infrastructure. But a change in attitude towards flats became increasingly necessary to maintain a *pied-à-terre* in the capital. The mansion block met this need and its nomenclature helped smooth over the stigma of flat dwelling. Impressive architectural designs signalled wealth, and spacious common access areas provided the necessary distance between dwellings. For bachelors and unmarried women in particular, the idea of renting a modern mansion flat became increasingly popular. Not untypically for London housing, these were rented rather than owned. Albert Mansions 1867–70 is one of the earliest examples designed by James Knowles on the newly constructed Victoria Street. Richard Norman Shaw, who as we have seen was never afraid to experiment with housing types, planned Albert Hall Mansions in 1876. The development was situated on Kensington Gore adjacent to the Royal Albert Hall and opposite Hyde Park. It comprised separate blocks to reduce the financial risk involved in speculating on this novel building type, and this approach proved successful. There were regional variations in the attitude towards flats. As we noted earlier in this chapter, from the 15th century onwards in Edinburgh Old Town terraces of ten- or eleven-storey blocks of flats, known as tenements, with communal entrances and staircases built in sandstone or granite were a form of housing for a number of social classes.

Across Britain, the living conditions of most of the urban poor deteriorated. Even when housing was built by industrialists for their workers the intentions were not always philanthropic. Terraces of houses were cheaply built on narrow roads with some constructed back to back, meaning they only had windows at the front. Overcrowding was inevitable, as the houses were small for the number of occupants, with only four rooms on two floors. The consequent lack of air circulation together with no water or sanitation meant conditions were unhealthy. In the 1960s and

1970s attempts were made to improve the housing of the urban poor with the rapid construction of tower blocks, which became a predominant feature of urban townscapes. This new high-rise living was intended to be utopian, but in reality, vertical slums frequently replaced their horizontal predecessors. Notably, tower blocks built for private sector housing benefited from better materials, construction, and maintenance, and continue to meet the needs of their wealthy occupants. By contrast, many of the local- authority-owned tower blocks were badly designed, with little understanding of the needs of working-class occupants. They were also often poorly constructed and inadequately insulated, in part due to cost cutting. These factors, together with many technical problems, including lifts being out of service, made life difficult for residents. The aesthetic might have pleased devotees of brutalism and modernism with the acres of unarticulated, repetitive concrete. But most importantly the street, which had been the main artery of former neighbourhoods and the social networks they contained, was destroyed. And there were no green spaces. Only two decades later, many local authority tower blocks had been demolished as they were not longer fit for purpose. This was due in part to the somewhat ironic fact that concrete was erroneously believed to be low maintenance and their overall poor condition was exacerbated by a lack of general upkeep. These tower blocks were replaced with low rise buildings or housing estates.

Park Hill in Sheffield is an exceptional example of these 'streets in the sky' (Figure 16). The area had comprised back-to-back housing, including two- or three-storey tenement buildings arranged in a grid. Residents used shared privies that were not connected to mains drainage and standpipes supplied water to up to a hundred people. By the 1930s the local authority recommended its complete demolition, noting that the houses were 'by reason of disrepair or sanitary defects unfit for human habitation, or are by reason of their bad arrangement, or the narrowness or bad arrangement of the streets, dangerous or injurious to the health of the inhabitants of the area'. But demolition was halted by World War II. In 1953 J. L. Womersley, Sheffield Council's city architect together with Jack Lynn and Ivor Smith produced the radical design for the Park Hill Flats (1959–61). Its brutalist style was inspired by Le Corbusier's Unité d'Habitation and Alison and Peter Smithson's unbuilt schemes, most notably for Golden Lane in London, which included deck access (streets in the sky) to the individual flats. Park Hill flats were viewed as an architectural triumph, with brochures in several languages promoting the design published by the city council. However, they did little to meet the needs of their various occupants and quickly became unpopular. Unlike many contemporary high rise housing projects Park Hill was structurally sound and to the consternation of some was listed at Grade II in 1998. In recent decades a public–private partnership had funded the renovation of the flats. Their upmarket specification combined with the growing fashion for city-centre living in re-used architecture, whether originally domestic or commercial, made Park Hill a commercial success, albeit for a different kind of resident.

I want to end this chapter with a sort of anecdote. Two of the questions I am asked most frequently as an architectural historian are 'why did tower blocks fail?' and 'what do you think of tower blocks?' In answer to the first question, it is possible to cite some of the evidence I have presented in this chapter. Flats in tower blocks, for example, lack privacy and a street, and can undermine the notion of 'home' we have explored in this chapter. Moreover, local authority housing frequently suffered from shoddy materials and construction techniques, which compounded the unsuitability of this kind of dwelling. And there is an absence of nostalgia in their austere often brutalist concrete designs, which are not necessarily appealing to the general public. But a modernist aesthetic could lend itself well to a properly maintained block of urban *pied-à-terres* for the wealthy during the week—their 'own front door' can be found outside of a city centre. Indeed, high

16. Park Hill Flats, Sheffield (1959–61).

density living is now popular in urban environments—we need only think of the proliferation of high rise developments in our city centres. Property developers who renovate blocks of flats (including ex-local authority properties), convert disused industrial or commercial buildings, or produce new-builds, use the word 'apartment', as it connotes a more exclusive dwelling. My response to the second question is usually a question: 'what is the architectural difference between a high rise tower block of the 1960s and a high density "executive" urban apartment or loft?' The answer lies partly in the financial circumstances of the occupant and partly in the nature of ownership. But sometimes, it is easier not to admit I am an architectural historian.

Chapter 4
The British abroad

When did Britain's architectural dialogue with the world begin? We might initially think British architecture in a global context is primarily a concern of the period beginning with the British Empire, and especially the 19th century. But the porosity between British architecture and the rest of Europe is a longstanding tradition, and Britain's international horizons had already expanded substantially by the end of the 17th century. Arguably, then, it is the 18th century and not the subsequent one that established Britain's architectural relationship with the world. Whatever starting point we choose, Britain's imperial and colonial past remains a dominant factor. How then do we address this? In this chapter I focus on three major themes: the influence of foreign architecture on British design; how architecture was used to project Britain to the world; and the influence of British architecture and architects abroad. We will consider on what terms British architects and patrons have engaged with the wider world and, importantly, some of the unexpected consequences of these interactions.

At the beginning of this book, we saw how Lincoln Cathedral is indicative of the architectural porosity between Britain and France as far back as the Middle Ages. And we have already encountered the wide sphere of European influence during the Elizabethan period, not least through the ever-increasing number of treatises on classical architecture, especially from the Netherlands and Italy. The developments in printing in the 18th century led to the increased availability of well-illustrated treatises published by British and European architects; the latter often available in translation. Some of these texts were the result of the popularity of European travel, especially the Grand Tour, which included many of the architectural sights and sites of Europe. The veneration for and adoption of classical architecture has been covered in Chapter 2 on 'The love of the past'. My interest here is in what these global architectural horizons tell us of Britain's view of itself in relation to the world. This is evident in the ways in which Britain projected its identity through design, and the influence of British architecture and architects overseas. But we begin by considering how the ever-expanding British exploration and colonization of the world influenced architectural design in Britain; the ways in which Britain's architectural horizons grew, and the effect this new knowledge had on design.

Expanded horizons—new pasts and other presents

Travel in Europe and the Mediterranean littoral is frequently presented as travelling through the past. As we have noted, the European past was experienced at first hand by the many 18th-century travellers. Men and women followed the established itineraries of the Grand Tour, with the sights and sites of Italy, especially Rome, as the primary destination. In the latter part of the century, alongside Naples, Pompeii, and Herculaneum, excursions to Greece expanded both the geographical spread of the Grand Tour and tourists' engagement with the past. The archaeological excavations of many hitherto largely inaccessible sites unearthed a past that was previously unknown. From the mid-18th century, travellers' horizons expanded further as they ventured East to visit the Ottoman Empire, China, India, and Egypt. Direct experience of these previously little-known lands led to fresh encounters with, and interpretations of, ancient and modern cultures. Knowledge of this new past and new present, specifically the art and architecture, was disseminated to a broad range of publics through prints and lithographs, complemented by scholarly tomes and surveys. But the 'East', used here in its broadest constituency, was often seen as something exotic, a novelty that did not challenge the cultural supremacy of the West.

A good starting point for a consideration of the architectural dialogue between East and West is the architect Sir William Chambers (1723–96). Chambers, who was a leading light in the neoclassical movement, is perhaps best known as a rival of Robert Adam. But there is another side to Chambers' practice that removes him from the orthodoxies of Greek and Roman architecture. Chambers was born in Gothenburg, Sweden, to a Scottish merchant father. Aged 17, he entered the service of the Swedish East India Company and completed three separate voyages to China in the 1740s, where he proved to be a keen student of Chinese architecture, interior decoration, and landscape design. On his return to Europe, he studied architecture in Paris and then in London. This training combined with his first-hand experience of China prompted Chambers to publish three treatises, including *Designs of Chinese Buildings, Furniture, Dresses, Machines and Utensils* in 1757, containing detailed information of Chinese architecture and design. Chambers reputation was made through a combination of his publications and his designs for the grounds at Kew Gardens 1757–62, including the Pagoda (Figure 17). Although he went on to rival Robert Adam as a leading neoclassical architect, his importance for making Chinese design available to a broad public should not be underestimated.

Chambers' designs and publications are indicative of the burgeoning taste for Chinoiserie across Europe that had been encouraged by the expansion of trade with East Asia from the 17th century onwards. This fashion was at its height in the latter part of the 18th century and continued in Britain until the start of the Opium Wars in the late 1830s, albeit on a reduced scale. The style

17. The Chinese Pagoda, Kew Gardens (1757–62).

was in fact more generic and fanciful than Chambers' attempts at accurate recreations of Chinese design. Indeed, 'Chinoiserie' was an all-purpose term encompassing not only China but also Japan, Korea, South-East Asia, India, and Persia. Chinoiserie was different from the adoption or adaptation of classical architecture, where the principles of design were studied, interpreted, and importantly were revered. The European view of the 'East' or 'Orient' both homogenized and eroticized the diverse aesthetics of the distinctive civilizations in Asia to present a fabricated ideal of beauty without order.

Chinoiserie mostly influenced the design of manufactures and interiors, although alongside the Pagoda at Kew there are notable examples of garden design and architecture. Henry Keene's design for a Turkish tent was part of the garden architecture for Painshill

Park in Surrey *c.*1760. Indian architecture was adapted to country house design—for example at Sezincote (1805) by Samuel Pepys Cockerell. Cockerell had worked as a surveyor for the East India Company although he never travelled to India and his knowledge of Mughal architecture was gained through the medium of drawings and engravings. But perhaps the Royal Pavilion at Brighton (1815–22) is most typical of this kind of generic misinterpretation of the 'Orient'. John Nash was commissioned by the Prince Regent, later George IV, to redesign and greatly extend his Marine Pavilion, which he used primarily for sybaritic pleasure. The building is known as both the Royal Pavilion and the Brighton Pavilion. It was built in three stages, with work beginning in 1787. Nash's Indo-Islamic exterior misappropriated Mughal, Islamic, and other generic 'Oriental' elements to present a wilfully phantastic aesthetic (Figure 18).

I will return to the issue of cultural appropriation later on, but here I want to focus on the critics of Chinoiserie. The classical, Palladian architect Robert Morris objected to the style as it 'consisted of mere whims and chimera, without rules or order, it

18. **The Royal Pavilion, Brighton (1787).**

requires no fertility of genius to put into execution'. But stronger views were expressed about the perceived lack of reason which it was claimed came from a world that was predicated on hedonism and was therefore both morally ambiguous and feminine. Chinoiserie is then a problematic style—it represents at once the cultural appropriation of a fictitious notion of the 'Orient' in Britain, and indeed elsewhere in Europe, coupled with racial and misogynistic critiques of the aesthetic. There is no doubt that the discovery of and encounters with these new pasts and new presents usually led to them being fetishized. But there are ways in which they also worked to disrupt architectural orthodoxies that were founded on an idealized European past.

Disrupting the classical European ideal

Classical architecture is usually seen to be both metaphorically and physically predominantly 'white'. But, in the 18th century, knowledge of architecture beyond Europe did disrupt some of the canonical orthodoxies of classicism and the roots of Western civilization. Here I want to explore how certainties about European culture, and specifically its architecture, were unsettled with regard to its racial origins, the use of colour, and more broadly notions of modernity. My point is not to deny the appropriation of cultures beyond the European envelope. Rather it is to highlight how these encounters could also open up fissures in the master narratives of Western culture. These might signal ways in which the binaries embedded in the narratives of colonizer and colonized could run in parallel to a circular flow of influence and reception.

By the latter part of the 18th century, travellers began to venture as far as Egypt. Up until this point knowledge of Egyptian sources was at best sketchy, gleaned mostly from publications of varying accuracy, including, for example, Benoît de Maillet's *Description de l'Égypte* (1735), and Richard Pococke's *A Description of the East and Some Other Countries* (1743). The superficial, exoticized use of Egyptian motifs based mostly on these sources can be found in the work of architects and designers such as William Chambers and Robert Adam during the latter part of the 18th century. The first systematic study of Egyptian antiquities, *Voyage dans la Basse et la Haute Égypte pendant les campagnes du Général Bonaparte* (Journey to Lower and Upper Egypt during the Campaigns of General Bonaparte) of 1802, was undertaken by the French archaeologist Dominique Vivant Denon, who was part of the scientific expedition that accompanied Napoleon Bonaparte's military invasion of Egypt 1798–9. Its popularity was immediate—two editions in English were published in the same year, fuelling the *goût d'Égypte* (Egyptian style) in Britain and beyond. This cultural appropriation of ancient Egypt as manifested in the *goût d'Égypte* is as problematic as the homogenization of Asia we encountered in the taste for Chinoiserie.

In Britain the *goût d'Égypte* ran in parallel with the Napoleonic Wars; it signalled the expansion of the British Empire and the defeat of Britain's long-time enemy, the French, at the Battle of Nile (1805) and finally at Waterloo (1815). The Egyptian Hall on Piccadilly, London (1812) was one of the first buildings in the Egyptian revival style but it was a pastiche, appropriated for novelty not accuracy (Figure 19). The hall was commissioned by William Bullock as a museum to house his collection, which had little to do with Egypt, largely comprising curiosities brought back from the South Seas by Captain Cook. The incongruity between museum and collection speaks for itself. Perhaps a more serious engagement with Egypt was to be found in the Egyptian Room at Thomas Hope's Duchess Street Mansion, London, which was accessible to the visiting public. The remodelled room included the display of original Egyptian sculpture placed alongside furniture designed by Hope in an Egyptian manner. Hope published details of his house in his influential book *Household Furniture and Interior Decoration* (1807). The room was intended to demonstrate the importance of the ancient Egyptians to the

19. The Egyptian Hall on Piccadilly, London (1812).

origins of Western culture. And this is a point worth exploring in more detail.

My interest here is in how the 'discovery' of ancient Egypt disrupted European and more specifically British ideas about its history, civilization, and culture. The revival and identification with the Classical world went hand-in-hand with the rejection of the immediate medieval past and set new parameters for the notions of cultural supremacy and of modernity. And we have seen this in, for example, the development of the country house in the 18th century, where classical design was viewed as modern. Increased knowledge of Greek architecture fuelled the Greco-Roman controversy about the superiority of either Greek or Roman architecture and this fed into debates about the relative supremacy of the ancients or the moderns.

The Romans found a champion in Giovanni Battista Piranesi, who was also very influential in Britain. His *Della Magnificenza ed Architettura de' Romani* (*On the Grandeur and the Architecture of the Romans*) of 1761 expounded his main thesis that the Romans had learned about design not from the Greeks, as British and French scholars argued, but from the earlier inhabitants of Italy, the Etruscans. Piranesi contested that Etruscan design was in turn derived from the Egyptians. In making this argument, he was asserting that Europe's visual culture was rooted in a civilization that lay outside its geographical borders in a different continent: Africa. The non-European basis of architecture and design did not find favour as it challenged the notion of European superiority. This was characterized in Johann Joachim Winckelmann's 1755 major work *Gedanken über die Nachahmung der griechischen Werke in der Malerei und Bildhauerkunst* (*Reflections on the Painting and Sculpture of the Greeks*), which asserted that the beginnings of European art (including architecture) lay in ancient Greece. Winckelmann established a Eurocentric chronology of the evolution of art which has remained largely unchallenged.

These debates also influenced architectural education in the early 19th century when Sir John Soane was professor of architecture at the Royal Academy. Architecture had been taught as an art alongside painting, drawing, and sculpture at the academy since its inception in 1768. Architectural instruction was delivered in a series of annual lectures, given to the architecture students, which were also open to royal academicians. Soane came down firmly on the side of the superiority of contemporary architecture over the achievements of the ancients. And this view was expressed in his lectures, giving him the opportunity to influence future generations of architects, as well as his contemporaries. Soane never visited Egypt but benefited from Denon's and Piranesi's work that showed ancient Egypt disturbed normative ideas about European architecture. In his first lecture in 1809 he sought to outline the origin of civil, military, and naval architecture, with an emphasis on first principles. Here we can see his view of ancient Egyptian architecture as being both the essence of architecture and proto-modern and how it fitted into the broader history of architectural theory and practice. There was then, for Soane, something in ancient Egyptian design that disrupted both the accepted chronology of European architecture and its roots in Greco-Roman tradition. The essence of architecture and the principles of modernity were to be found not in Europe but in Africa.

The world in colour

Engagement with Egypt shows us how British architecture was conceived of as metaphorically 'white'. But what about the physicality of its whiteness? The architecture of ancient Greece and Rome was experienced by travellers as appearing to be made from plain stone or marble. And this trend was followed in Renaissance architecture, where architects such as Palladio developed building techniques to replicate the perceived aesthetic of the ancients. And as we have seen, 18th-century country houses and townhouses in Britain were built from stone or faced in stucco to emulate stone. But, if you will forgive the question, was the absence of colour in antique architecture such a black and white issue?

The increased exploration and excavation of ancient architecture in the early 19th century revealed that buildings, and indeed statues, were originally highly coloured. Owen Jones provides us with an excellent example of how polychromy was introduced into British architecture as a modern phenomenon. After studying at the Royal Academy schools, Jones wanted to develop a modern style, unique to the 19th century, that would be distinct from the aesthetics of neoclassicism and the Gothic Revival. In pursuit of this idea, he followed the now expanded route of the Grand Tour (1832–4) to explore the question of polychromy in architecture. His studies of Greek, Egyptian, and Turkish architecture confirmed that colour had been integral to design. But it is an example of Moorish architecture in Europe itself that proved to be the important catalyst in his thinking. Jones undertook a detailed study of the Alhambra Palace in Granada. He published his finding in the highly influential *Plans, Elevations, Sections and Details of the Alhambra* (1842–5). Importantly, Jones explored the new technique of chromolithography to ensure his book supplied accurate representations of the colours used in the design of the palace. The intricate tilework at the Alhambra encouraged Jones's interest in contemporary developments in flat patterning, geometry, and abstraction. His designs for tiles attracted the attention of Prince Albert, who was committed to design reform. He invited Jones to be involved with the Great Exhibition of 1851—which was intended to project a modern British identity to the rest of the world. We will return to this in the next chapter.

British architecture abroad

We have seen in Chapter 2 that colonialism is inextricably linked with domestic architecture in Britain, especially the country house. And this extends to the usually classical-style plantation houses of the slave-owning landed elite in the West Indies. Similarly, housing in the United States, especially the eastern seaboard, followed the example of British townhouse design, as well as ideas about town planning. Here I am interested in the ways in which Britain projected its national identity in a global context. My question is: how did Britain's military expansion and colonialism influence its architectural relationship with the rest of the world?

The East India Company began trading with India in the 17th century. In 1690 their presence was consolidated in the amalgamation of three villages in Bengal to form present-day Kolkata (then known as Calcutta). The colonists changed their role from traders to the new rulers and Kolkata was the British capital of India from 1773 to 1912. Lord Robert Clive, whom we have already encountered at his country house Claremont, was the first British governor of Bengal and helped establish British dominance across India. By 1765 the corruption of the officials in the East India Company led Clive to describe Kolkata as 'the most wicked place in the universe'. And there has been recent speculation as a consequence of the corruption and wholesale looting of India overseen by Clive that his death may have been by his own hand. In terms of its architecture, Kolkata has been described as the city of palaces and conversely as the city of dreadful night—a derogatory phrase used by Rudyard Kipling. Exploring the city's architecture between these two bifurcated views allows us to examine how British identity was projected in a colonial setting and the role of architecture in this colonizing process. Kipling's opinion typifies the colonial standpoint that Indian architecture lacked the qualities that were considered important in Europe in terms of design and urban planning. This assessment was used to justify the imposition of public buildings that made Britain's imperial position as a ruler visible and this architecture represented the empire itself. The adoption of some indigenous architectural elements also worked to emphasize British political and cultural dominance. Mughal architecture was especially popular, as the Mughals were the previous rulers or conquerors of India. Esplanade Row was perhaps the most notable part of the new urban plan of Kolkata. It provided a grand urban vista that was deployed as a symbol of power. And by 1780 the splendour of the public buildings, including Government House and the High Court, as well as private dwellings, caused a resident of the city, Mrs Fay, to remark that it 'seems to be composed of palaces'.

The pattern of constructing a notion of inferiority or otherness in the culture and society of the country that was being colonized was a familiar model across the British Empire. What role did architecture play in this process? To explore this question, I will remain with examples from India. It is noteworthy that many British architects did not visit India but instead sent designs which were executed by military engineers. Untypically, Thomas Roger Smith did visit India in 1864 to design exhibition buildings in Mumbai (then known as Bombay), but the project was abandoned. Nevertheless, other buildings were erected from his designs, including the Post Office and British Hospital at Mumbai. Smith is perhaps better known for his remarks at the Society of Arts, in 1873, where he argued that European styles were the most appropriate for the British Empire and its public buildings. A contrary view was posited by William Emerson, who stated that Indo-Saracenic styles should be used on such buildings, in India. Their exchange was part of an ongoing debate about the most appropriate style for colonial buildings. The results of these stylistic debates can be found in Mumbai and include the Convocation Hall or Cowasji Jehangir Convocation Hall and Rajabai Clock Tower (1869–74) at the University of Mumbai, both designed by the well-known Gothic Revival architect Sir George Gilbert Scott. Like the majority of his contemporaries, Scott did not visit India and his designs were realized at arm's length from their architect. The Convocation Hall has a quasi-ecclesiastical aesthetic, whereas Scott modelled the Rajabai Clock Tower on the clock tower of the Palace of Westminster in London. In addition, Scott's designs, including that for the Midland Grand Hotel at St Pancras Station in London may well have influenced the Victoria Terminus railway station (1887), now known as Chhatrapati Shivaji Terminus. The station was designed in an Italian Gothic style by Frederick William Stevens, an architectural engineer who lived in Mumbai.

The British decided to move the capital of their Indian Empire from Kolkata to Delhi in 1911. Sir Edwin Lutyens, known for his imaginative adaptation of traditional architectural styles for modern buildings, including houses, war memorials, and public buildings, led a group of architects to create a new district: New Delhi. Alongside an urban layout comprising axial roads such as the Rajpath (formerly Kingsway) and Janpath (formerly Queensway), the new capital had to retain a substantial area of green space. The plan comprised several important administrative buildings and monuments as focal points (Figure 20). Perhaps the best known are Rashtrapati Bhawan (formerly known as the Viceroy's House), and India Gate (formerly known as the

20. Rashtrapati Bhavan with the Jaipur Column, New Delhi (1911).

All India War Memorial). The example of India shows us the role that architecture and urban planning played in expressing Britain's assumed right to rule during a period of intense colonialist expansion. And there is some circularity here as words such as 'bungalow' (originally meaning a house in the Bengali style) and 'veranda' (a Hindi word that may itself have been derived from Portuguese explorers and colonizers in India) are now part of the architectural lexicon, but their colonial derivation might remain unnoticed. Were there other ways in which empire was exported?

Exporting empire

As Britain's overseas colonies expanded in size so did the need for a range of building types to meet the requirements of the growing population. We have already seen how the design of the Georgian terraced house was adopted on the eastern seaboard of North America. Doubtlessly, the proliferation of builders' or pattern books facilitated the migration of this distinctive form of housing.

21. St Martin-in-the-Fields (1722–6), London.

But what of the other kinds of architecture that are germane to
the colonial urban fabric? Here I focus on places of worship and
particularly the influence of St Martin-in-the-Fields (1722–6),
which stands in Trafalgar Square, London (Figure 21). Although it
was by the Scottish Catholic architect James Gibbs, it was one of
the first churches specifically designed to accommodate the needs
of 18th-century Anglicans both at home and across the British
Empire. In 1728 Gibbs published his well-illustrated *A Book of
Architecture* which was intended for 'Gentlemen as might be
concerned in Building, especially in the remote parts of the
Country, where little or no assistance for Designs can be
procured...which may be executed by any Workman who
understands Lines'. It became one of the most influential
pattern books in British architecture and Gibbs's design for
St Martin-in-the-Fields proved exceptionally popular and was

replicated across Britain and its colonies. Notably here the design formed the basis of the many Episcopalian churches in North America.

Empire was also exported in prefabricated form. We have already seen how new materials and construction techniques influenced the design of buildings such as the Crystal Palace. Alongside iron and glass, wood could also be prepared in a factory setting—as seen, for example in the Portable Cottage produced in 1837 by Henry Manning, a London carpenter, for export to Australia. But from the 1830s, corrugated iron was one of the most commonly used materials. It was painted or galvanized for use in dwelling houses, churches, hotels, clubs, as well as warehouses. By the mid-19th century, cast iron was widely used for store fronts and architectural details such as columns, capitals, stairs, and decorative railings on a variety of buildings. As part of the colonial conquest of South Africa in the latter part of the 19th century, entire towns of iron houses were sent from Britain to facilitate the building of settlements and the consequent cultural and political domination.

My final example pre-empts our consideration of international exhibitions and world's fairs in the next chapter. These mega-events included exhibitions that were staged across the British Empire. Their ephemeral nature means they have left a very limited architectural trace. But there were some exceptions. The Royal Exhibition Building in Melbourne, Australia (1879–80), by Joseph Reed of Reed and Barnes was built to host the Melbourne International Exhibition in 1880–1. It was followed by the even larger Centennial International Exhibition in 1888. It was then repurposed to house the formal opening of the first parliament of Australia in 1901. The design was eclectic, drawing on many past styles. Like the Crystal Palace, the Royal Exhibition Building is an example of a vast cathedral of knowledge. The enormous structure, including a great hall of over 12,000 square metres (c.40,000 square feet), is in the shape of a Latin cross. The large dome, constructed from cast iron and wood, was modelled on Florence Cathedral, while the main pavilions were influenced by the Rundbogenstil—a blend of Byzantine and Romanesque revival that was particularly popular in Germany.

British architects abroad

Over recent decades British architects have become increasingly important players on the world stage. In some ways it is difficult to discern what, if anything, is British about their designs, as they speak to an international currency of architecture that meets the needs of corporate, governmental, or private patrons. Of course, this does not detract from the quality or significance of the landmark buildings themselves. That said, it is important to note that the increasingly collaborative nature of design in terms of its remit and developing relationship to art and engineering has led to a distinct change in the practice of architecture. Moreover, the increasing volume of staff in offices across the world has led to a greatly expanded number of projects produced by collaborative (often multidisciplinary) teams. But many of these designs are still assigned to a single architect, rather than being a group effort. Inevitably, given the volume of possible examples and that this is a very short introduction to British architecture, I will be highly selective in my choices. But my focus here is not so much the architecture, but rather the different kinds of indicators of the esteem in which British architecture is held. Leading on from this, I consider the increasing diversity to be found in the British architects whose work enjoys a global presence. Perhaps predictably, I begin with the 'triumvirate' of British architecture: James Stirling, Norman Foster, and Richard Rogers. Doubtlessly they are some of the best-known British architects in recent times, but how are they viewed abroad?

Prizes and awards can be seen as a kind of litmus test of the prestige of British architects and how British architecture, both at home and abroad, is viewed in the global arena. The Pritzker

Architecture Prize, an international award often dubbed the Nobel Prize for architecture, aims 'to honour a living architect or architects whose built work demonstrates a combination of those qualities of talent, vision and commitment, which has produced consistent and significant contributions to humanity and the built environment through the art of architecture'. As I write, the British architect David Chipperfield has become the fifty-second winner of the prestigious award for his work that spans four decades. The jury commended him for 'steering clear of trends' while having a 'commitment to an architecture of understated but transformative civic presence'. These qualities are perhaps typified in Chipperfield's Hepworth Wakefield art gallery (2011).

James Stirling was the first British winner only two years after the Pritkzer's inception in 1979. The jury's citation sums up Stirling's contribution as 'a leader of the great transition from the Modern Movement to the architecture of the New—an architecture that once more has recognized historical roots, once more has close connections with the buildings surrounding it, once more can be called a new tradition'. Of particular note was his work in three countries—Britain, Germany, and the United States. In his Seeley Library (1968) at the University of Cambridge, Stirling made prominent use of prefabricated elements and precast concrete panels. The main interior feature of the building is the Reading Room, with capacity for 300, which is topped by an impressive glass roof. All the corridors and other accommodations are ranged around this space. The vast Reading Room connects to the enquiry area and the book stacks radiate from this space on two levels. There is also a control area for the various measures to moderate the climate and lighting within the building in response to the weather and time of day. The library had existed since the 19th century and the new building was part-funded by the endowment made in 1897 by the historian John Robert Seeley, who defended the repressive activities of the British Empire. As we have noted elsewhere, the meaning of architecture for a range of publics can change over time. In common with other buildings

22. Neue Staatsgalerie, Stuttgart (1984).

and artworks that celebrate the British Empire there has been a petition to rename the Library. Stirling later went on to design the Sackler building (originally an extension) at the Fogg Museum, Harvard University, and the Neue Staatsgalerie, Stuttgart, both in 1984 (Figure 22). The design of the Neue Staatsgalerie echoes the neoclassical style of the adjacent Alte Staatsgalerie, as well as making reference to the Altes Museum in Berlin, the Guggenheim Museum in New York, and the Pantheon in Rome, as well as some of Stirling's own unbuilt projects. The building is constructed from travertine and sandstone in classical forms, which contrast with the industrial pieces of green steel framing system and the bright pink and blue steel handrails. The most prominent feature is a central open-top rotunda housing the sculpture garden. The juxtaposition of modernist and classical elements has prompted some critics to claim the Neue Staatsgalerie as the beginning of 'postmodernism' in architecture. The Neue Staatsgalerie and the Sackler building continue to receive international acclaim for their architectural innovation, although the patronage of the Sackler is now not without its controversies.

In 1999 the prize was awarded to Norman Foster. Like Stirling, who had encouraged Foster early in his career, he was aware of the historical roots of architecture. Foster was praised by the Pritzker jury for his ability to produce remarkable solutions for urban settings, especially the juxtaposition of contemporary and ancient architecture, as seen in his sensitive placement and design of the Carré d'Art, a cultural centre next to the Maison Carré, Nîmes, a Roman building (begun towards the end of the 1st century BCE). His transformations of more recent historic buildings include the Reichstag in Berlin and the new Great Court of the British Museum. The original 19th-century design for the British Museum by Robert Smirke (1823) comprised galleries ranged around an open quadrangle. The quadrangle later became the site of the circular Reading Room of the British Museum Library, designed by Robert's brother, Sidney (1857). The library was housed at the museum until its move to a purpose-built structure by Colin St John Wilson in 1997. The quadrangle, including the Reading Room, was redeveloped and became the Queen Elizabeth II Great Court, commonly referred to simply as the Great Court (2000) (Figure 23). The principal feature of the design is the vast tessellated glass roof, engineered by Buro Happold and built by Waagner-Biro, covering the entire quadrangle, including the Reading Room, which is now a museum. Foster has also produced many grand mega-projects, including the world's largest air terminal, and the much-acclaimed Hong Kong and Shanghai Bank, both in Hong Kong. More recently the Ilham Tower development (2016) brings together a variety of spaces for living and working in the heart of Kuala Lumpur. The fifty-eight-storey, 275 metres (902 feet) high tower has a compact urban footprint and is one of the tallest mixed-use developments in the city. The internal layout responds to the need for flexible, column-free spaces to accommodate its mixture of functions. And the tower's diamond-shaped plan affords views of key city landmarks and the façades tilt away from the morning and evening sun to reduce solar gain.

23. The Great Court, British Museum, London (2000).

Richard Rogers, perhaps best known for his striking design for the Centre Georges Pompidou in Paris (1971–7), was awarded the Pritzker in 2007. The Pompidou was followed by Terminal 4, Barajas Airport in Madrid (1997–2005), which also demonstrates Rogers's fascination with the building as a machine. His headquarters for the insurance brokers Lloyd's of London (1978–86) established Rogers's distinct style of architecture. The design typifies his own brand of architectural expressionism, where the services for the building, such as ducts and elevators, are located on the exterior to maximize space in the interior. Lloyd's is located on the former site of East India House in Lime Street, London. What may be a more surprising juxtaposition is the installation of the original dining room of Bowood House in Wiltshire, designed in 1763 for the 1st Earl of Shelbourne by Robert Adam, on the top floor of the new building. It had been moved from Bowood in 1956 to become the interior of the boardroom of the previous Lloyd's headquarters. The Lloyd's building itself became a quasi-historical artefact when in 2011 it received Grade I listing, as it was 'universally recognised as one of the key buildings of the modern epoch'. It remains one of the youngest structures to obtain this status and adds an additional layer of richness to the development of 'The List' we encountered in Chapter 2. However, its innovation of having key service pipes routed outside the walls has led to very expensive maintenance costs due to their exposure to the elements.

The jury citations for the Pritzker have a familiar tone for most of the laureates, and our triumvirate are no exception. Stirling was 'a prodigy for so many years—as a leader of the great transition from the Modern Movement to the architecture of the New'. Foster's 'ability to produce remarkable solutions' is described as 'brilliant'. Similarly, 'Key Rogers projects already represent defining moments in the history of contemporary architecture'. Does this language remain the same when the laureate breaks the mould of the (usually white) male architect?

My example here is Zaha Hadid, a British, Iraqi-born architect and a woman of colour. In 2004 she became the first and to date the only woman architect to be awarded the Pritzker prize. The jury's citation is distinctive, noting that her

> architectural career…has not been traditional or easy…Her path
> to worldwide recognition has been a heroic struggle as she
> inexorably rose to the highest ranks of the profession…Ms. Hadid
> has become more and more recognized as she continues to win
> competition after competition, always struggling to get her very
> original winning entries built. Discouraged, but undaunted, she has
> used the competition experiences as a 'laboratory' for continuing to
> hone her exceptional talent in creating an architectural idiom like
> no other.

To be clear, I am not simply pointing fingers of blame at the Pritzker. My point is rather that the terminology used in this citation is indexical of the bias, both conscious and unconscious, in the assessment of architects who do not conform to the established norms. And this is something we have encountered throughout this book—especially in Chapter 1.

Hadid's built architecture is beyond doubt world leading in its originality and significance. Early work includes the Vitra Fire Station (1993), the LFone in Weil am Rhein, the Mind Zone in the Millennium Dome, and the critically acclaimed Rosenthal Center for Contemporary Art in Cincinnati, Ohio (2003). More recently, Hadid's work has generated disapprobation and admiration in equal measure. The London Aquatics Centre was originally designed in 2004 as a public swimming pool, but when London won the bid for the 2012 Olympics it was repurposed to be part of the new Olympic Park. The considerable adjustments included the addition of temporary spectator wings to accommodate the anticipated audience of 17,500. The design proved flexible enough to accommodate the transformation from public pool to Olympic facility and now it has reverted to a public pool. The undulating roof that mirrors the riverside landscape of the site is the distinctive feature familiar to many of us. Indeed, Hadid is sometimes called 'the queen of the curve'. We see this unique and structurally challenging design element in much of Hadid's work—notably the Heydar Aliyev Centre in Baku, Azerbaijan, and Qatar's Al-Wakrah stadium. The latter, which was designed for the 2022 World Cup football tournament, has courted controversy. According to Hadid, the design was inspired by the sails of Arab *dhows*. By contrast, others choose to disregard the architect's words and say what the form of the building represents is female genitalia. We have not time to ponder the Freudian meaning of this interpretation of a building designed by a woman by (mostly) male critics. But I will pose the question: has there ever been so much fuss about the many towers that are designed by male architects?

My interest here is not so much the bias in the views of Hadid, it is more what it tells us of how comfortable norms are disrupted and what happens as a consequence. You might permit me to add my own experience as a woman who has punched through a number of glass ceilings—that the issues of equality, diversity, and inclusivity are not as simple as dissembling the binaries of normative and non-normative. Let me explain.

We have Hadid's own view of the problems she had encountered as an architect.

> I don't like tough times but I seem to get them all the time. It's a triple whammy—I'm a woman which is a problem to many people, I'm a foreigner—another problem, and I do work which is not normative, which is not what they expect. Together it becomes difficult.

Hadid neatly encapsulated the established binaries of the white, Western male in the power relationships that have been inherent in the practice, theory, and history of architecture. Eva Jiřičná confirmed that Hadid 'hated' being considered a 'female architect' rather than just an 'architect'. In some ways this is problematized by Frank Gehry's description of Hadid shortly after she died in 2016 as 'one of the guys'. He added: '[That's] sexist in its own way I suppose. I don't mean it that way. She was undaunted by all the stuff that would be against a woman coming into a field at that level. She didn't pay attention to it…She was very confident.'

To my mind Gehry, perhaps unintentionally, reinforces the binary gender assumptions inherent in the term architect. At what point does an architect become 'daunted' rather than 'undaunted', 'attentive' rather than 'inattentive', 'unconfident' rather than 'confident'. Why are the values Gehry sees as positive assets inherent in the word 'architect' with all its masculine associations? And, conversely, why does the modification of the word by the adjective 'woman' diminish the idea of the architect? But if we follow Hadid's and Gehry's viewpoint and write women into the masculinist narratives of architecture, do we miss an opportunity to expand our understanding of the word architect?

The future is bright

We have arrived at the internationally renowned 'star' architects at the end of our journey through British architecture. And they are very different from the anonymous master masons and amateurs we encountered at the beginning. We also noted in Chapter 1 that the practice of architecture in Britain remains dominated by white men. Recently the profession has begun to become more diverse and inclusive, which goes some way to it being more in step with the population as a whole, and I will return to this point in the final chapter. But I realize that in concluding this part of the book on this note I risk appearing as if I have bundled together architects from ethnic minorities. But my intention is to show that the category of architect, and with it British architecture, has opened up considerably in recent decades. In what ways have architects from ethnic minorities contributed to this important shift in British architecture at home and abroad?

The British/Ghanaian architect David Adjaye received the Royal Gold Medal in 2021, approved personally by the late Queen Elizabeth II, for his significant influence 'either directly or indirectly on the advancement of architecture'. Adjaye challenges the established norms for the design of certain building types by juxtaposing different functions as well the blurring the delineation of interior and exterior space. Like many British 'star' architects Adjaye's best-known work is abroad. One of his first international commissions was the Museum of Contemporary Art Denver, which opened in 2007. The building was designed to dissolve boundaries between the exterior spaces of the city and the naturally lit interior galleries of the museum with the use of exceptionally large windows. This was followed by the equally innovative Moscow School of Management Skolkovo (2010), where the traditional campus layout is transformed into spaces that encourage student interaction. The Aishti Foundation (2015)

24. National Museum of African American History and Culture, Washington DC (2009–16).

in Beirut, Lebanon, combines, perhaps unexpectedly, the practices of gallery going with shopping.

The imperial past is addressed in David Adjaye's National Museum of African American History and Culture in Washington, DC (2009–16) (Figure 24). The museum is the result of a centuries-long struggle to recognize the importance of the Black community in the social fabric of American life and as such it rethinks the role of what a civic institution should be. This is achieved through Adjaye's design, which offers new modes of user experience and engagement while accommodating an evolving collection and wide range of artefacts. In this way, cultural narratives and identities address aspects of the human condition and the positive value inherent in creating a forum for multiple interpretations of America's history and demography. The structure operates simultaneously as a museum, a memorial, and a space for cross-cultural community building that provide a deeper understanding of our past and current contexts to inform our future. The design of the museum has three principal features that signal its crucial function. It is wrapped in an ornamental bronze-coated aluminium lattice that is a historical reference to African American craftsmanship. The density of the pattern can be modulated to control the amount of sunlight and transparency into the interior. The south entry is composed of the porch and a central water feature. As an extension of the building out into the landscape, the porch creates an outdoor room that bridges the gap between the interior and exterior.

Architecture and activism powerfully combine in the work of the British Ghanaian-born Elsie Owusu. She was a partner for ten years with Fielden+Mawson, where she was co-lead architect for the UK Supreme Court, a redevelopment of an existing building. Owusu is director of JustGhana, a company based in Britain to promote investment, sustainable development, and constructive social engagement in Ghana. Her engagement with the developing world also includes a directorship of ArchQuestra, 'formed to provide the best of British architecture, art and engineering to support emerging economies'. Owusu has also been a significant agent of change in the architectural profession in Britain. In 2015 she was among the twelve 'RIBA role models' to support inclusivity and diversity in the profession. Two years later, Owusu launched, with the Stephen Lawrence Charitable Trust, the RIBA+25 campaign to advance diversity in architecture. This coincided with the twenty-fifth anniversary of the murder of Stephen Lawrence, who had hoped to become an architect. As we noted in Chapter 1, architecture is one of the least diverse professions in Britain. This was emphasized in 2015 by the *Architects' Journal* where it was pointed out that 94 per cent of architects self-identified as white, and only 4,000 of RIBA's 27,000 chartered architects were women. Owusu's '+25' initiative, supported by many including David Adjaye, Alison Brooks, and Richard Rogers, resulted in her being joined by eleven other architects as members of the RIBA governing council. Owusu's unsuccessful bid, launched in 2017, to be the first Black female president of RIBA was supported by more than seventy chartered architects including Sir David Adjaye, Owen Luder, Deborah Saunt, and Yasmin Shariff. However, in 2022, Nigerian-born Muyiwa Oki was elected the first Black president of RIBA, following on from the first non-white/person of colour to hold the position, the Indian-born Sunand Prasad (2007–9). Oki is remarkable not only for this achievement but also because, at 31, he is the youngest president in RIBA's history. His election signals not only an important shift towards diversity and inclusion but also a concerted campaign by early-career architects who were determined to elect one of their own to the eminent post rather than an establishment figure who had founded their own practice and served on many RIBA committees. Adjaye, Owusu, and Oki are indexical of the beginnings of a more diverse and inclusive definition of the idea of the architect and of British architecture both at home and abroad. And this leads me to my final question: what language does British architecture speak?

Chapter 5
What language does British architecture speak?

Throughout this book we have seen the different languages that architecture can speak to a range of publics and how meaning can change over time. The language of architecture can be found, for example, in the use of a specific style, as we have seen in the adoption of Palladian style in country house design as an expression of elite supremacy or the modernism of post-World-War-II housing and its philanthropic principles. Building types can also convey a distinct message or meaning through their function but they may not look the same. A good example here is the notion of 'authority', as expressed in the Edwardian classicism of Aston Webb's façade which was added to Buckingham Palace in 1913 or the Scottish Parliament Building (2004) by the Spanish architect Enric Miralles, which aimed to achieve a poetic union between the Scottish landscape, its people, its culture, and the city of Edinburgh (Figure 25). The buildings look very different but each effectively articulates royal or governmental rule respectively. Civic authority is defined by function, for example in the medieval and Tudor city gates that acted as physical boundaries to towns and cities, including the City of London. By contrast, Britain's colonial expansion prompted the use of both architectural style and function as a means of stamping authority and the assumed right to rule.

Form and function combine in a variety of ways and we see this in the ways in which civic and town halls became part of the

25. Scottish Parliament Building, Edinburgh (2004).

19th-century British urban streetscape. They also connoted
change as, for example, in the case of Belfast City Hall (1906)
(Figure 26). The need for an impressive civic building was
identified when Belfast was awarded city status by Queen Victoria
in 1888 in recognition of its rapidly expanding linen, rope-making,
shipbuilding, and engineering industries. Indeed, Belfast
Corporation used their profits from the gas industry to pay for the
construction of the building, which was designed by Sir Alfred
Brumwell Thomas in the Baroque Revival style, and built in
Portland stone. We see also how a range of vocabularies were used
to articulate the purpose of town halls as emblems of local
autonomy and its incumbent bureaucratic processes. Notable here
are the classically inspired New Town Hall in Leith (1829), the
neo-Gothic of Manchester Town Hall (1877), or the High
Victorian eclecticism of Leeds Town Hall (1858). But their
common purpose was to serve the local community, often
providing, for instance, public reading rooms or libraries. We see
how, perhaps encouraged by their civic predecessors, large

26. Belfast City Hall, Belfast (1906).

corporations have also expressed their power through landmark buildings that encourage us to feel some benefit through attractions that are integral to their structures. We have encountered this already in the Lloyd's Building, which includes a museum. Recently the London Mithraeum, an ancient Roman temple that was excavated and moved in the 1950s, was returned to near its original site and housed in Norman Foster's Bloomberg London Building (2017). The Mithraeum occupies a space 7 metres (23 feet) below ground level that also houses a collection of contemporary art.

My intention here is not to look back across the chapters of the book or to list an array of new examples in what must inevitably be a selective survey of British architecture to underscore the points I have just made. The chapters have demonstrated the variety of ways in which architecture can be used to articulate particular agendas and how these may be accepted or not by a diverse range of publics. Instead, I want to focus on how architecture can also be used to project a British identity both at home and abroad. My focus is international exhibitions, as these show us how architecture morphed from being an expression of empire into an agent of soft power. How does architecture operate as a barometer of Britain's changing views and engagement with the world?

The Great Exhibition of the Works of Industry of All Nations (1851) was housed in a temporary structure in Hyde Park, London. An international competition failed to produce a workable design to meet the competing needs of an impressive, large-scale but inexpensive, easily dismantlable structure that was to have minimal impact on the natural environment of the park. Eventually, Joseph Paxton's design was inspired by greenhouse construction, comprising a modular system of cast iron columns and timber roof beams spanned by glass (Figure 27). The design made the most of the new, mechanized, labour-saving methods of production, and the speed and efficiency of construction was startling. The mostly glass structure earned the name Crystal Palace, whilst the interior had a cathedral-like atmosphere including a vaulted transept tall enough to cover the trees growing in the park that needed to be preserved. The vast scale of the building, which covered 800,000 square feet (*c.* 75,000 square metres), with a symbolic length of 1,851 feet, was made possible by

27. **The Crystal Palace, London (1851).**

the new constructional techniques. Its modern design was intended to signal Britain's supremacy to the rest of the world. As we have noted, Owen Jones was responsible for the interior decoration of the building. His radical paint scheme for the interior utilized only the primary colours blue, red, and yellow, which he combined with Gothic and Moorish influences to emphasize the constructional elements in a novel way. The building opened to great acclaim and was visited by six million people—three times the contemporary population of London. And the articulation of the interior using colour was the result of Jones's interaction with architecture that originated from outside Europe, which he used to emphasize the modernity of Paxton's design. Despite its original temporary status, the Crystal Palace was dismantled and resited in Sydenham in 1854, where it remained as an attraction and an exhibition venue until it was destroyed by fire in 1936.

The interior arrangement of separate courts became the method for organizing the national displays of the ninety-three countries represented—including many from the British Empire. Notably, the Indian Court was the centrepiece of British imperial representation, with a substantial contribution of items from the East India Company. It may be that the Indian Court was intended to affirm or bolster imperial rule. This was a period of uncertainty in Anglo-Indian relations as only six years later the Indian Rebellion, also known as the Sepoy Mutiny, marked a significant uprising against the East India Company, which was in effect the sovereign power of the British crown. The East India Company was finally dissolved in 1874.

The Great Exhibition was the first international exhibition of its kind, comprising a comprehensive display of modern manufactured goods from Britain and its empire and beyond, housed in a purpose-built modern building. The profits from the Great Exhibition were used to develop the South Kensington Museum (now the Victoria and Albert Museum). Jones had met Henry Cole, the museum's first director, whilst working on the Crystal Palace and through this association he became a pivotal figure in the development of modern design in 19th-century Britain. Jones's *The Grammar of Ornament* (1856) promoted his theory of design and selected examples of what he judged to be good ornament from other cultures and periods, although some of his knowledge was gleaned from secondary sources. Alongside his well-illustrated publications, Jones's theories of modern design were publicized through his lectures at the Society of Arts and at the Government School of Design, which also offered courses to women. Following on from the Great Exhibition, architectural exhibitions and World's Fairs became a global phenomenon. Notably, many of these included sections devoted to women designers. How was British architecture used to present national identity to an international audience at home and abroad?

Exhibiting British architecture

The enthusiasm for large-scale exhibitions, many of them with overbearing imperialist agendas, continued in Britain. But there was little in the way of architectural innovation. However, by the 1930s the modern movement had permeated British architecture and once again exhibitions and the projection of national identity provided an important catalyst for innovation and novelty. Despite the forward-looking design, empire remained a strong theme and we see this in the Empire Exhibition, Scotland, of 1938 which was unofficially known as the British Empire Exhibition, held at Bellahouston Park, Glasgow. It was an opportunity to boost the Scottish economy, which was recovering from the depression of the 1930s. The exhibition attracted twelve million visitors. Arguably, the architecture demonstrated a more progressive attitude to imperialism and the empire in the modern buildings designed for the exhibition as well as the displays themselves. It was planned by the Scottish modernist Thomas S. Tait, who was required to employ younger Scottish architects in his team of nine. These included Basil Spence and Margaret Brodie, a graduate of

28. The Palace of Engineering, Empire Exhibition, Glasgow (1938).

Glasgow School of Architecture. She had entered the School in 1926 as a student of the newly introduced BSc (Architecture) course which was conducted jointly with the University of Glasgow. Brodie was admitted ARIBA in the late 1930s (as an associate not a full member of RIBA). Of the many British pavilions, the Palace of Engineering and Palace of Industry were the two largest, whilst countries from the empire contributed their own national pavilions (Figure 28). The 300 feet (91 metres) high Tower of Empire was the dominant architectural centrepiece, with viewing platforms that provided a panoramic view of the whole site and beyond. It was constructed in only nine weeks from the steel beams and corrugated steel used in the local shipbuilding industry. The tower was intended to remain as a permanent monument after the exhibition, but it was demolished in July 1939.

A tonic to the nation

The Festival of Britain (1951) marked the centenary of the Great Exhibition and was envisaged as being on a grander scale than its predecessor. Held in the aftermath of World War II, it aimed to showcase collective and individual British achievements and like its predecessor it was to be a 'visible sign of national achievement and confidence'. Importantly, unlike other national exhibitions, this was a nationwide event—comprising a series of exhibitions and associated activities around the country. It was intended to be a means of tempting traders to Britain to boost the export market, to encourage large numbers of foreign visitors to invigorate the economy, and to demonstrate Britain's recovery to the world. The initial scope of the Festival was scaled back due to the financial constraints and competing priorities of postwar reconstruction. Nevertheless, the main site received over eight million visitors during its five-month run. Despite the supposed political neutrality, the Festival did set out the broad parameters of the social democratic agenda for modern Britain. Significant here is the state's use of architects and town planners as part of the agenda for building a better Britain. We have also come across this agenda, with its emphasis on progress and modernity, science and planning, in Chapter 2.

Alongside its regional locations, the main site of the Festival was the South Bank of the Thames in central London. Once again, the structures were mostly temporary and the emphasis was on modernity rather than tradition. The Skylon and the Dome of Discovery designed by Ralph Tubbs gave a futuristic appearance to the site (Figure 29). The interior of the Dome was rather disappointing, as the galleries designed using the modernist's favourite material, reinforced concrete, were spoiled by the overbusy cluttered display. The only permanent building was the Royal Festival Hall, designed by architects Leslie Martin and Robert Matthew, as London County Council's contribution to the Festival. It is one of Britain's earliest postwar public buildings and its modernist style, as seen in the use of concrete construction and large areas of glass, pointed the way to a brighter future. The interior is an example of 'democratic' design comprising wide open foyers for visitors to mingle, and bars and restaurants to

29. The Festival of Britain, London (1951).

provide a meeting place for all. And there were no 'bad' seats in
the auditorium. The Great Exhibition / Festival of Britain format
was invoked again to celebrate the third millennium CE. The focal
point was the Millennium Dome designed by Richard Rogers and
engineered by Buro Happold, which is reminiscent of the Dome of
Discovery. As with the Crystal Palace, the combination of
innovative design and pioneering engineering produced a
landmark building whose entire roof structure weighs less than
the air it contained.

British architecture as soft power

The enduring legacy of International Exhibitions and World's
Fairs is their celebration of Western colonialism. A change of
name signalled a change in tone of these global festivals when in

1967 the International and Universal Exposition in Montreal was promoted under the name Expo 67. But, disappointingly for present-day readers, the theme of 'Man and his World' indicated there was still progress to be made. British architecture did respond to the new challenges presented by a world Expo. But national projection remained at the heart of the British pavilions, which were to showcase excellence in design. The pavilions were selected by a government-run competition which included a rubric for the qualities necessary in a winning design. Here we see how the jingoistic imperialism of the 19th-century exhibitions and World's Fairs was gradually eclipsed by a more ambassadorial and promotional tone—a kind of architectural soft power. And this impacted on the pavilions themselves, which have become multisensory works that explore the interface between architecture, art installation, and sculpture. But the past casts a long shadow and we find in many of the recent British pavilions echoes of the Great Exhibition in terms of issues of the relationship to nature and strategies for re-use. I would also contest that the notion of British industry and culture as spectacle is a common theme, albeit expressed through different forms of architecture and technology.

We see the beginning of this transition in the projection of British identity abroad in the Expo '92 in Seville, whose theme was 'The Age of Discovery'. The government's competition brief was for proposals to emphasize Britain's leadership in the technology and service industries, which also conveyed an image of cultural excellence. The winning design, by Nicholas Grimshaw and partners, referenced both the Crystal Palace and the Festival of Britain, as seen in the off-site prefabrication of major building elements, mostly in Britain, together with a strategy for re-use either of the whole pavilion or its components. The large cathedral-like rectangular structure in steel and glass measured 65 metres × 32 metres, with a height of 25 metres (213 feet × 104 feet × 82 feet) from lower ground floor to roof. It was entered via a bridge over an external lake. The design followed local traditions to counter the intense heat of Seville. This included shading and awnings and the use of water to cool the air. The East Wall, the main public face of the pavilion, was glazed for its entire length, with water pumped from the lake pouring continuously down the outside to maintain a maximum glass temperature of around 24°C (75°F).

The ecclesiastical theme continued in Thomas Heatherwick's award-winning design for the Shanghai Expo 2010, colloquially known as the Seed Cathedral. Confronting rather than addressing the Expo's theme of 'Better City, Better Life', it explored the relationship between nature and cities. In contrast to the other pavilions that, perhaps predictably, concentrated on high tech, the British pavilion worked with the Kew Gardens' Millennium Seed Bank Partnership. The design explored the interface between architectural and sculptural form to create an organically shaped structure of approximately 25 square metres (213 square feet) composed of 60,000 slender transparent fibre optic rods, each 7.5 metres (24.5 feet) long. The organic, non-static design is emphasized by movement of its optic 'hairs' in the wind. The tips of these undulating rods that faced the interior of the structure contained seeds, thus confronting the visitor with an array of small display cases. The rods also drew daylight into the interior whilst, at night, light sources inside each rod allowed the whole structure to glow. The interior surrounded the visitor with an immersive experience that transformed the binary oppositions of architecture and the collection it houses and displays.

Immersive experiences that engage with the natural world and address issues of sustainability have remained dominant themes in the projection of British identity at subsequent Expos. Here we see how architecture, art practice, and technology can overlap. The 2015 pavilion for the Milan Expo was the Hive, a celebration of Britain's honeybees by the artist Wolfgang Buttress. The 17 metres (56 feet) high distinctive mesh frame was constructed from 170,000 aluminium parts and 1,000 LED lights. True to its heritage, the Hive is a sustainable structure and is now appropriately situated in Kew Gardens. This was followed by Asif Khan's the Yurt for the 2017 Astana Expo. It was an innovative CGI panorama of a living landscape. Although the themes of nature and sustainability are clearly to the fore here, I cannot help thinking about the early-19th-century Dioramas and Panoramas that emerged as places of urban entertainment. Examples of these could be found in the upmarket new urban development of the Regent's Park in London. These short-lived building types provided the viewer with an early form of immersive experience through lighting effects and hand-painted vistas. The 2020 Poem Pavilion by the artist and set designer Es Devlin has the appearance of a conical giant wooden instrument, with each elemental part exhibiting words input by the visitors before they stepped into the interior Choral Space, where they were cocooned in a soundscape, with the music featuring voices and sounds from all over the world. The Poem Pavilion demonstrates how Britain is working to provide future, sustainable solutions. To this end, the building is constructed from cross-laminated timber—a sustainable alternative to steel and concrete—and has a thermal labyrinth as part of its cooling system. The Hive, the Yurt, and Poem Pavilion speak a very different language from the architecture of their 19th- and early-20th-century predecessors. Here we see how architecture becomes a statement of soft power and a means of expressing national identity as well as British cultural and social aspirations in a global context. And importantly, like David Adjaye, Elsie Owusu, and Muyiwa Oki, they signal a more diverse and inclusive definition of the idea of the architect and of British architecture.

And finally

I began this book with two important questions. What is architecture? And what makes it British? And to explore these questions we have looked at everything from bicycle sheds and cathedrals to country houses and tower blocks, and public buildings and exhibition architecture. We have considered what is understood by the term British architecture and how it has developed and changed as regards its indigenous and foreign influences, how it is distinctive across the regions and nations, and how its meaning may change over time as it speaks to a broader, more diverse public. Alongside this we have traced the evolution of the idea of the architect, the different practices of design and building, and the opening up of British architecture and architects as more diverse and inclusive categories. What we mean when we say British architecture will always remain in flux. But to my mind this ensures that it remains vital and relevant.

Further reading

Chapter 1: What do we mean by British architecture?

Dana Arnold, *Reading Architectural History* (2002)
Howard Colvin, *Biographical Dictionary of British Architects 1600–1840* (1954)
Nikolaus Pevsner, *Outline of European Architecture* (1943)
Spiro Kostof, *The Architect: Chapters in the History of the Profession* (1977)
Sumita Singha, *Thrive: A Field Guide for Women in Architecture* (2023)

Chapter 2: The love of the past

Dana Arnold, *The Georgian Country House: Architecture, Landscape and Society* (1998)
John Summerson, *Architecture in Britain 1530–1830* (1954)
Roger Dixon and Stefan Muthesius, *Victorian Architecture* (1978)
Victoria Perry, *A Bittersweet Heritage: Slavery, Architecture and the British Landscape* (2022)

Chapter 3: There's no place like home

Alice T. Friedman, *House & Household in Elizabethan England: Wollaton Hall and the Willoughby Family* (1988)
Jill Franklin, *The Gentleman's Country House and Its Plan 1835–1914* (1981)
John Summerson, *Georgian London* (1978)

Stefan Muthesius Miles Glendinning, *Tower Block: Modern Public Housing in England, Scotland, Wales, and Northern Ireland* (1994)

Chapter 4: The British abroad

Andrew Ballanytne and Andrew Law, *Tudoresque: In Pursuit of the Ideal Home* (2012)

Becky Conekin, *The Autobiography of a Nation: The 1951 Festival of Britain* (2003)

Elaine Harwood, *Mid-Century Britain: Modern Architecture 1938–1963* (2021)

T. J. Boisseau and Abigail M. Markwyn, *Gendering the Fair: Histories of Women and Gender at World's Fairs* (2010)

Chapter 5: What language does British architecture speak?

Andrew Ballantyne, *Architecture: A Very Short Introduction* (2002)

Clare Nash, *Contemporary Vernacular Design: How British Housing Can Rediscover Its Soul* (2019)

Colin Cunningham, *Victorian and Edwardian Town Halls* (1981)

Lynne Walker and Elizabeth Darling, *AA Women in Architecture: 1917–2017* (2017)

Index

For the benefit of digital users, indexed terms that span two pages (e.g., 52–53) may, on occasion, appear on only one of those pages.

Index

Index

DESERTS
A Very Short Introduction
Nick Middleton

Deserts make up a third of the planet's land surface, but if you picture a desert, what comes to mind? A wasteland? A drought? A place devoid of all life forms? Deserts are remarkable places. Typified by drought and extremes of temperature, they can be harsh and hostile; but many deserts are also spectacularly beautiful, and on occasion teem with life. Nick Middleton explores how each desert is unique: through fantastic life forms, extraordinary scenery, and ingenious human adaptations. He demonstrates a desert's immense natural beauty, its rich biodiversity, and uncovers a long history of successful human occupation. This *Very Short Introduction* tells you everything you ever wanted to know about these extraordinary places and captures their importance in the working of our planet.

www.oup.com/vsi

GLOBALIZATION
A Very Short Introduction
Manfred Steger

'Globalization' has become one of the defining buzzwords
of our time - a term that describes a variety of accelerating
economic, political, cultural, ideological, and environmental
processes that are rapidly altering our experience of the world.
It is by its nature a dynamic topic - and this *Very Short
Introduction* has been fully updated for 2009, to include
developments in global politics, the impact of terrorism, and
environmental issues. Presenting globalization in accessible
language as a multifaceted process encompassing global,
regional, and local aspects of social life, Manfred B. Steger
looks at its causes and effects, examines whether it is a new
phenomenon, and explores the question of whether,
ultimately, globalization is a good or a bad thing.

www.oup.com/vsi

LANDSCAPES AND GEOMORPHOLOGY
A Very Short Introduction
Andrew Goudie & Heather Viles

Landscapes are all around us, but most of us know very little about how they have developed, what goes on in them, and how they react to changing climates, tectonics and human activities. Examining what landscape is, and how we use a range of ideas and techniques to study it, Andrew Goudie and Heather Viles demonstrate how geomorphologists have built on classic methods pioneered by some great 19th century scientists to examine our Earth. Using examples from around the world, including New Zealand, the Tibetan Plateau, and the deserts of the Middle East, they examine some of the key controls on landscape today such as tectonics and climate, as well as humans and the living world.

www.oup.com/vsi

THE INDUSTRIAL REVOLUTION
A Very Short Introduction
Robert C. Allen

The 'Industrial Revolution' was a pivotal point in British history that occurred between the mid-eighteenth and mid-nineteenth centuries and led to far reaching transformations of society. With the advent of revolutionary manufacturing technology productivity boomed. Machines were used to spin and weave cloth, steam engines were used to provide reliable power, and industry was fed by the construction of the first railways, a great network of arteries feeding the factories. Cities grew as people shifted from agriculture to industry and commerce. Hand in hand with the growth of cities came rising levels of pollution and disease. Many people lost their jobs to the new machinery, whilst working conditions in the factories were grim and pay was low. As the middle classes prospered, social unrest ran through the working classes, and the exploitation of workers led to the growth of trade unions and protest movements.

In this *Very Short Introduction*, Robert C. Allen analyzes the key features of the Industrial Revolution in Britain, and the spread of industrialization to other countries. He considers the factors that combined to enable industrialization at this time, including Britain's position as a global commercial empire, and discusses the changes in technology and business organization, and their impact on different social classes and groups. Introducing the 'winners' and the 'losers' of the Industrial Revolution, he looks at how the changes were reflected in evolving government policies, and what contribution these made to the economic transformation.

www.oup.com/vsi

UTILITARIANISM
A Very Short Introduction
Katarzyna de Lazari-Radek and Peter Singer

Utilitarianism is arguably the most influential secular ethical theory in the world today. It is also one of the most controversial, clashing with many conventional moral views.

In this *Very Short Introduction*, Peter Singer and Katarzyna de Lazari-Radek provide an authoritative account of the nature of utilitarianism. They explore the utilitarian answer to the question of whether torture can ever be justified, focusing on the utilitarian view that only happiness is of intrinsic value, and analysing the importance of utilitarianism in the world. They discuss how it is a force for new thinking on contemporary moral challenges such as global poverty.